Every Single Ministry

How to Start or Revitalize A Christian Single Adult Ministry

Max Holt & Doug Stephens

MaxHolt Media

HOLT & STEPHENS

EVERY SINGLE MINISTRY

Max Holt Media
303 Cascabel Place, Mount Juliet, TN 37122
www.maxholtmedia.com,   max@maxholtmdia.com
On facebook at www.facebook.com/maxholtmedia

Disclaimer: There is no intention in this work to inappropriately reference any names, persons, businesses, places, events and incidents mentioned herein. Any such references have been preceded by permission-to-use from the appropriate source.

SCRIPTURE quotations are from the Holy Bible, *New International Version*, Copyright © 1973, 1978, 1984 by International Bible Society

Cover design by: © Max Holt Media

ISBN 13: 978-0-9966104-3-8

Acknowledgements

We want to thank all of the single adults who have impacted our lives over the years, especially those who were a vital part of S.P.L.A.S.H. (Single People Loving And Serving Him), the Single Adult Ministry at Hilldale Baptist Church in Clarksville, Tennessee. Their honesty and openness about the needs in their lives encouraged us to rise to a level of leadership that found ways to meet those needs.

We also want to thank our wives for their patience and support as we ministered in the lives of thousands of single adults.

INTRODUCTION

There are various books, manuals, video & audio lessons, etc., available and marketed as *How To..* publications for starting a SAM or revitalizing one that is struggling. This Leader's Edition is designed to help churches quickly begin ministry with single adults of all ages by providing a simplified format for inexperienced leaders, even in the smallest churches. For organizations with existing SAMs this kit will help revitalize or refocus the ministry to move more toward its intended purpose. Throughout this publication the use of the capital letters **SAM** refers to the phrase **Single Adult Ministry,** whether it is one small class or a large group with several classes and ministries**.**

Feel free to make photocopies of the *fill-in-the-blank* portions of this Kit to use as working copies for your organization. That will ensure that you will always have a Master Copy to make other copies to use for changes. Please refer other organizations to Amazon.com for their own copy of this copyrighted kit.

Throughout this publication you will find references to and excerpts from a publication entitled, **The Single Adult Ministry Solution Kit (**ISBN 0-8054-9835-4)**.** It is a non-copyrighted and is no longer in print, but you may find used copies on the Net. **The SAM Solution Kit** is not essential but would be helpful if you can find one. There are other SAM Leadership Books that have been developed and published by various organizations. An Internet search will assist you in locating such publications. This S.A.M. Manual uses a *start-from-scratch, fill-in-the-blank* format, which will be useful to the smallest churches or will serve as a reminder of the basics for larger churches with established SAMs. **Section 19** near the back of this kit will list many of the related resources.

So, just fill in the blanks. But, be sure to do all the recommended actions or it will be just another 'booklet' with all the blanks filled in, without the resulting ministry. We've all done too much of that! If you or your church cannot afford the recommended resources, try cooperating with an Association of churches or a few neighboring churches to share the cost. Keep one important truth in mind as you use this manual: Any SAM is most successful as a partnership ministry where two or more people share leadership and work together to determine purpose and direction. Individually-led ministries will usually have a narrow focus and will suffer or fail if the leader is absent or leaves. Your goal should be to have shared leadership from the beginning, regardless of the size of your ministry.

CONTENTS

CHECKLIST

Use this checklist to help keep track of your progress in implementing a SAM in your church. Put a checkmark following each item to indicate that you have completed that task. For your own records you may want to write the date accomplished. It will serve as a reminder for you to keep pressing forward on your mission to present Christ to every single adult within the influence
of your church and your SAM.

1. PRAYER TEAM _____

2. PURPOSE & VISION _____

3. TARGET GROUP _____

4. CHURCH LEADERSHIP SUPPORT _____

5. NARROW YOUR TARGET GROUP _____

6. LEADERSHIP _____

7. FACING LEADERSHIP CHALLENGES _____

8. BUDGETING _____

9. DECIDING WHERE, HOW AND WHEN TO START ____

10. ADVERTISING _____

11. START DAY! _____

12. SPECIAL NEEDS _____

13. DOCUMENTING YOUR MINISTRY _____

14. CREATIVE IDEAS _____

15. INVOLVING SINGLES IN THE CHURCH _____

16. EVALUATE YOUR SAM _____

17. EMPOWERING SINGLE ADULTS _____

18. MEANINGFUL MINISTRIES _____

19. OTHER SAMINISTRY RESOURCES _____

1. PRAYER TEAM

James 5:16, "Therefore confess your sins to each other and pray for each other so that you may be healed. The prayer of a righteous man is powerful and effective." The most important element in the beginning of any SAM is PRAYER. Call your Association or State denominational office and ask their Single Adult person to pray for you and to offer any assistance in starting your ministry. Your church office should have the number. List it here and in Enclosure 6.

Asso. Person _____ Phone _____

Email _____

State Person _____ Phone_____

Email _____

Form a Prayer Team of at least three people who see the vision of a ministry designed to reach single adults for Christ. There should be at least one single adult on the team. Recruit only those who are spiritually serious and have evidence of an on-going prayer life and those who will be consistent in their partnership with the team. All team members should make a commitment to both team prayer and individual prayer. **List the team** here and in Enclosure 6.

Name: _____ Phone _____

Email _____

Name: _____ Phone _____

HOLT & STEPHENS

Email _____

Name: _____ Phone _____

Email _____

Name: _____ Phone _____

Email _____

2. PURPOSE & VISION

PURPOSE:

Why should you do ministry with the single adults in your area? The basic answer is found in Matthew 28:19-20, *"Therefore go and make disciples of all nations, baptizing them in the name of the Father and of the Son and of the Holy Spirit, and teaching them to obey everything I have commanded you. And surely I am with you always, to the very end of the age."*

Notice that it said to make **disciples** first, not just converts. Notice the detail...it said to **baptize** (after they become disciples) and to **teach** them to **observe all things**...in other words, teach them how to live a Christ-like life. All too often churches will state their purpose as *"getting people saved."* But the scripture is clear; we have a responsibility to **mentor** or **teach** them **how** to live as Christians.

This is a big area of failure in most churches we have observed. The Pastor can't teach the detail needed from the pulpit. As you will see in the following pages, single people are certainly part of "**all the world**.*"* Effective ministry to any group does not happen by accident; it happens when we *on purpose* commit ourselves and our resources to it. Philippians 2:1-2 says, *"If you have any encouragement from being united with Christ, if any comfort from his love, if any fellowship with the Spirit, if any tenderness and compassion, then make my joy complete by being like-minded, having the same love, being one in spirit and* **purpose.***"*

You must know your PURPOSE for doing ministry with single adults. What do you want your SAM to accomplish? The church must know the purpose and the single adults who will participate must know the purpose. People will respond to a ministry if they know **why**...if they understand the GOAL...if they know WHAT you are trying to accomplish. Work with your church leaders to first determine the Purpose of the church. Why does it exist? What is its target group? What is it trying to accomplish?

When you know the purpose of the church, then you can you define the purpose of your SAM, ensuring that it does not contradict the purpose of the church. (If you have The Single Adult Ministry Solution, Leader Manual, refer to Solution 2 on page 61. This method is very helpful.) Take your time as you work on defining your PURPOSE. Brainstorm with others in the church, especially those who will be in the Single Adult Ministry. One group's Purpose was defined like this: "The purpose of our Single Adult Ministry is to, "Reach and teach young single adults about Jesus and their need for salvation. To help them find and pursue their calling in life as they grow into fully devoted followers of Christ."

If your church is surrounded by many apartment units, where the majority of the occupants are single parents, your purpose might read, "To share the love of Christ with single parents and their children, leading them to accept Him as Savior and grow as His disciples. To minister to their fellowship needs, feeling of community and recovery needs so that they can do meaningful ministry in the lives of others."

Notice the statements in those purposes that will require the SAM to design mentoring relationships and provide specific lifestyle training to singles. Remember, as the scope and dynamics of your ministry change you will need to review and maybe modify your purpose. **Write your Purpose** below.

Purpose of _____ **Church:** Our purpose is to…

_____

_____

_____
_____
_____

List names of those defining the purpose:

_____   _____

_____   _____

Purpose of our Single Adult Ministry:

Our purpose is to...

_____

_____
_____
_____
_____

List names of those defining the purpose:

_____   _____

_____   _____

VISION:

Our leadership mentor, Dr. John Maxwell, published a book entitled, "*The 21 Irrefutable Laws of Leadership.*" One law is the "*Law of the Buy-In*" It is summarized as, "People will buy-in to **you, before** they buy-in to your vision." That's why you have to nail-down your understanding of your purpose and vision.

VISION asks the question..."What can we *see* as the result *IF* we accomplish our purpose?" DREAM is a good word because it speaks of a deep *desire* to accomplish or achieve something. VISION has the same context *but* has at its foundation confidence born out of knowledge about the task at hand. Some people use the words VISION and GOALS to mean the same thing.

We use the word GOALS to mean those intermediate steps we want to accomplish as parts of the overall VISION. Let's say that there are 5,000 single adults in your ministry area. An appropriate VISION for your SAM would **NOT BE**, "We will reach and impact the lives of all 5,000 single adults during the next five years." That is not an appropriate VISION because it does not consider the Target Group of your ministry and does not take into account the limitations put on your SAM by physical and financial barriers. If 5,000 came, **where** would you put them? Do you have 5,000 empty seats now?

Certainly, your VISION must be based on faith but it has to be realistic and something that can actually be accomplished. It must take into account the financial condition of the church, the space available, the future building plans for the church, the staff support for your ministry, your plans to grow and expand your leaders, etc. If you have a *pie-in-the-sky* vision that isn't based on reality, your SAM will most likely not realize the Vision and experience discouragement among your Leadership Team. Your VISION shouldn't be based just on *numbers.* Part of it has to be directed at **changing lives;** seeing singles make lifestyle changes that reflect the spiritual excellence taught in your SAM.

Let's take a look at an **appropriate** VISION. If your PURPOSE is to reach the large group of Single Parents in your area, you might state your VISION like this: ***"Our vision is to see our Single Parent Ministry grow in attendance by 10% every year, to see 50% of those attending, who are unsaved, accept Christ as Savior and Lord; to see single parents become financially stable through wise decisions, to see 10% of those*** *attending commit to leadership and ministry each year and to see our Christian singles growing deeper spiritually and applying spiritual principles in their daily lives."*

How well you do your PURPOSE will determine how your VISION turns out.

Vision of our Single Adult Ministry:

Our VISION is:

_____

_____

_____

_____

_____

List names of those defining the vision:

_____   _____

_____   _____

NOTES:

3. TARGET GROUP

One of the biggest challenges of any ministry is defining WHO is in their target group and WHERE those people are. It is essential that you do the work in this area. Obviously you will begin with the single adults already in your church; there will always be a few. Remember, single adults are defined as, "*Those out of High School and older who are not currently married, whatever the reason.*"

From the beginning of your SAM encourage leaders to refer to those you reach as SINGLE ADULTS, rather than SINGLES. Most single adults do not take offense at the term *SINGLES*; it is used in secular society often. However, many church leaders view SAM as similar to the Youth Group; a group centered on activities and recreation. They will refer to groups in the church such as ADULTS, SINGLES, YOUTH and CHILDREN. This indicates to the church that single adults are NOT adults. But they ARE adults, with the same career and family concerns and responsibilities that married adults have.

The myths that single adults are *well off, have plenty of time, have no worries, do not care or contribute to the church, live a wild lifestyle, etc.,* simply are **not true**! Constantly remind church leaders that you are ministering to ADULTS, with most of the same ministry needs as married adults. Remind them that most Bible characters did their best ministry while they were single; the young adult David, the Apostle Paul and the greatest single adult of all, Jesus.

In your ministry, avoid using titles or class names that label people as *Divorced, Single Again, and Starting Over,* etc. Many churches have a separate College Ministry but there are many adults in that age range who do not attend college. Also, some single adult groups we've seen have members age 70 and older. So, be open to the needs of the single people of any age in your church.

Detailed national marital status statistics on age categories are at the web site: www.census.gov . Click on QUICK FACTS and then select your state. THEN, at the top of the page you can click on PEOPLE and find dozens of statistical lists. The two lists that may give you the most pertinent information are the HOUSING list and the MARRIAGE list. The Census Bureau is not as easy to interpret as we would hope, so you will have to carefully read all associated comments to correctly decipher the reports. Census Bureau definitions of the various categories are helpful and can be found at the following website:
http://cber.cba.ua.edu/asdc/households_families.html.

A printout of the HOUSEHOLD page from the 2010 US Census is attached as Enclosure 2. Our research has not yet revealed the details by state, but we are still looking. Using the HOUSEHOLDS Table and the MARITAL STATUS Table we estimate that there are 127,004,644 single adults in the country. We also find that 63% of them (79,625,958) are listed as Never Married. Only 21.3% (27,038,098) are divorced. Over one half of all single adults are under age 40. Your church leaders are probably unaware and will certainly be very surprised by these numbers.

Generally, age category characteristics have not changed much over the years:

20s – Most have never been married. The median age of first marriage these days is reported differently by various agencies but is approximately 26 for women and 28 for men. Many in their early 20s do not consider themselves to be single, especially if they are in an on-going dating relationship. They generally consider themselves to be Young Adults. Challenging economic times can cause these adults to wait longer to marry and result in many living at home with their parents, even after college graduation. Cohabitating relationships are common in this category.

Also, there is a growing number of never-married single parents in this category. Relationship issues are prevalent and these singles want quality honest guidance in this area. Few of these young adults see the need to formally *join* the church and will be content to enjoy the fellowship of the ministry without putting their names *on the dotted line*. **This category is the most difficult to reach!**

30s– A growing number of 30s have never been married. Most of the single parents with children still at home will be in this category. Divorces are prevalent in the 30s and continue to increase in the follow-on categories. Recovery ministries and childcare become important here. People in their 30s are looking for relationships in a co-ed group. Relationship training is very important because most divorcees will remarry. These people become more serious about spiritual things. Many new leaders will come from this group.

40s – Divorce rates increase in this category. Recovery ministries and childcare during activities become essential. Relationship training is very important because most divorcees will remarry. They better understand their need for the church, so Bible Study attendance and spiritual growth will increase. Many leaders will also come from this category.

50s - The highest divorce rates are in this category. The need for childcare decreases dramatically but the need for relationship training remains high. This category will have the highest percentage of adult children returning home. Finances become more of an issue, which makes low cost events more important. Widows and widowers increase here as well as the need for a Grief Recovery Ministry. Some in this category are becoming caregivers of elderly parents and lose flexibility to be active in a SAM.

60s – The need for childcare is all but gone as is the desire for relationship training. Widows and widowers increase dramatically here as well as the need for a Grief Recovery Ministry. More and more, this age group contains single grandparents who are raising their grandchildren. Many of these will need help from a single parent group. A lot of ministry workers and servants are in this category.

To find where the single adults are, in and near your church, there are several tools at your disposal. Start with your church. Your current records should give you a good idea as to who the single people are. Ask your administrator or record keepers to help with accurate data. Ask them to determine if guests who register are single. They should NOT ask guests if they are SINGLE. They will probably answer NO if they are dating, separated, divorced, engaged, widowed, etc. Instead, they should be asked, *"Are you married?"* Your *Activity* or *Bible Study* Registration Form should have a place to circle **Status**, with all the above choices in the list. Knowing the exact category of a person helps you design ministry to meet their needs. Ask the church to collect as much family information as possible on people, including social media contacts.

Make a list of single adults already in your church, even if they are in leadership positions on Sunday, which prevent them from attending a single adult Bible Study class. Single adult ministry is best begun through the foundation of Sunday School but it is NOT just about Sunday School; it is about ministering in the lives of all single people. Talk to other leaders who can help identify single people for you.

We'll discuss later about marketing your ministry to the single people in your church. List below, and in Enclosure 6, those single adults in your church who immediately come to mind as those who might be excited and willing to help start or grow your SAM. If they are leading in other areas, make sure they are listed in a class as *Associate* members so they will be contacted with information about activities. Make an effort to involve them in leadership in non-Sunday-School activities.

Name _____ Phone _____

Email _____

Name _____ Phone _____

Email _____

Name _____ Phone _____

Email _____

Name _____ Phone _____

Email _____

Name _____ Phone _____

Email _____

Use demographic reports to help define the single population of your immediate area. Your City Hall or County Clerk's/Parrish Office may have current statistics. Your State Denominational Office may provide a report more tailored to your needs. Ours does reports of pertinent data on people within a five-mile, ten-mile and fifteen-mile circle of our church. Ask yours for such a report.

The Census WEB Site will give details of your area but it requires careful reading to interpret the data. The way the Census Bureau categorizes the various segments of society is somewhat confusing and prevents us from determining an *exact* number of single adults but you can come very close to an accurate total by using all of the TABLES provided. Once you determine the potential number of single adults your church could reach it is time to develop a plan to do just that.

NOTES:

4. CHURCH LEADERSHIP SUPPORT

Your Pastor, deacons, elders and maybe other leaders will determine the direction that ministry will take in your church. These leaders are usually interested in church growth. Providing them the information about the ministry potential of the single adult population will help you compete for the time and resources at these leaders' disposal.

Most leaders do not know that about 50% of all ADULTS in America, ages 18 – 69, are single. It may be higher or a little lower in your area. They are very surprised to learn that **only** about 21.3% of all single adults are divorced and that most singles are younger, never-married adults! They will be impressed when you tell them the number of single adults already working in the church, providing leadership and ministry in many diverse areas. Some of those church leaders either have singles in their household or know some young singles. Ask them to refer singles to your new ministry.

Some leaders worry that single adult ministry will encourage divorce. Remind them that SAMs don't *cause* divorce; they help people *heal* from divorce and become productive church members who contribute to the ministries in the church. Also, the relationship training you will eventually offer will help prepare singles for marriage and help reduce the divorce rate. In the 15 years of SAM leadership at our church there were over 200 marriages. Although the County Divorce Rate was just over 50% for new marriages, the divorce rate for our whole group was under 20% (still too high but still good news.) However, the divorce rate for the 105 couples that went through pre-marriage counseling was less than 10%! We used a pre-marriage video series entitled, *"So, You're Getting Married?"* by H. Norman Wright, published by Grace Ministries. It is outstanding!

Encourage church leaders to also provide divorce prevention training for the married couples in the church. Marriage seminars, retreats and classes can help greatly. Write the names of the primary church leaders below, and in Enclosure 6, and lead your Prayer Team to pray for them. Begin to form a good working relationship with these leaders so they might see your heart for single adults. Seek opportunities to discuss with them the positive things about single adults in your church.

Pastor _____   Phone _____

Email _____

Other Staff _____ Phone _____

Email _____

Chairman of Deacons _____

Phone _____

Email_____

Finance Committee _____

Phone _____

Email_____

NOTES:

5. NARROW YOUR TARGET GROUP

As much as you would like to reach **every** single adult in your area it is unrealistic to think that you are capable of doing so. Even the largest and best-equipped ministries in the country do not reach all categories well. The demographics of the single adults already in your church may determine your starting group. If most are young adults, target them. If most are over 30 and divorced, then that will be your starting group. Your available leadership will also determine the target. John Maxwell, (www.johnmaxwell.com) Leadership Mentor and Founder of the INJOY Life Club says, "You can teach what you know but you will reach who you are." The **'Who you are'** refers to the *atmosphere* single people see when they come.

Example: If your teacher is a 40-year-old divorced single mother she will identify best with other single mothers whose ages are close to hers and her class will most likely consist of people like her. Leaders must work very hard to reach others outside their own demographic. If your class is led by singles it will work best as a partnership of two singles, each from a different category of life experiences. Quality Leadership Training, addressed below, can help that become a reality. We agree with John Maxwell; "Everything rises and falls on Leadership," (and we add, 'relationships').

Do not lead this ministry by yourself! You must partner with someone else who can be a prayer partner and can help with the challenges of leadership. The one thing we know for sure about a turtle on top of a fence post is, it didn't get there by itself; someone helped put it on top! You will succeed better when others help you on your journey upward. Be sure that the Team has single adults of all the categories in your Target Group, such as never-married, divorced, single parents, widowed, etc. This diversity will keep you from becoming too narrow in your focus. Work through the process and identify your Target Group below.

Target Group:

_____

_____

_____

_____

NOTES:

6. LEADERSHIP

You may be the Pastor of your church and you've realized that **if** you intentionally exclude single adults from church growth, that you are eliminating almost 50% of the adults from your church growth plan! So, you are committed to starting a SAM--Great! Or, you may be a married couple, a single parent, a divorced person, a college student or a never-married single adult with a desire to see the church reach out to the single people in your area. Great! This kit will help you.

But, remember this; you don't understand all single people, even if you are single. Never-married people do not understand divorcees. College students don't understand never-married 30-Something issues. We VMPs (very married people) do not understand most issues faced by single people. So, your only hope is to gather a team representing the various statuses of single adults and then practice shared leadership.

As mentioned earlier, everything rises and falls on leadership. Your main job is to begin to grow other leaders. We've heard it said that you should **never** try to grow a great SAM; rather, you should try to grow great people and let *them* grow a great SAM. The first leadership decision you must make is to commit *yourself* to grow personally as a leader. You must put people, seminars, resources and opportunities in your life, that help you climb to a higher level as a leader.

On a scale of 1 to 10, if your leadership ability is a 5, you will never lead anyone higher than level 5 with you. If you do the work to grow to a 7, you can grow other leaders to that level also. Make a commitment to keep growing as a leader. Never pass up an opportunity to be trained.

When possible, go to all conferences, seminars and Sunday School clinics available to you where leadership is taught. Call your Association or State Office and ask when the next training opportunity is scheduled near you. List it below and put it on your calendar. Ask other potential leaders to accompany you to the training. When affordable, purchase or ask your Church/Association to purchase, some of the Personal Growth materials listed in section **19: Other Single Adult Ministry Resources,** at the end of this booklet. Some are free! We recommend you take advantage of the resources available at www.johnmaxwell.com.

Training Opportunity

_____

Date_____ Time_____ Location _____

Everyone, including you, needs a Mentor; someone who is more skilled in leadership, to help monitor your progress, evaluate your leadership and make recommendations for improvement. Look for a Christian leader inside or outside the church who would agree to help you on your leadership journey. Do the work to grow as a leader.

You may wonder if married or single people should lead single adults. The answer is, YES! Marital status has little to do with the success of a SAM, regardless of size.

What matters are leadership ability and the passion to make a difference in peoples' lives. Recruit and accept only those leaders who will commit to the *work* necessary to lead or teach with excellence. Some ministries require specialized leaders. Divorce Recovery should only be led by a divorced or previously divorced person who **has recovered** from divorce.

DO NOT allow someone still suffering from the pain of a fresh divorce to lead a recovery class. A previously divorced, remarried couple can be excellent leaders. Single Parent classes should only be taught by current or previous single parents.

Career & College classes work best when led by an older more mature college student or married college graduates. You get the idea; leaders must be able to identify and empathize with those they lead.

At our church we required our leaders to sign a Leadership Covenant, agreeing to attend faithfully, be well prepared, maintain pure relationships, tithe, etc. A copy of the Leadership Covenant we used at Hilldale Baptist is provided as Enclosure 3. We encourage you to use it and modify it as you wish.

Some believe that covenants discourage leaders from committing to leadership. We have found that leaders are more committed and consistent when called to a higher level of expectations. Committed leaders will always rise to the level of excellence expected of them. We require all leaders to take a Spiritual Gifts Profile annually. As people grow spiritually, their gift-strengths change. The Profile was an indicator as to the effectiveness of our training. The Profile is free from Life Way Church Resources and can be found at: http://www.lifeway.com/Article/Pastors-spiritual-gifts-Help-your-people-discover-their-spiritual-gifts.

Right click on the link "Spiritual Gifts Survey by David Frances" and then select "Save Link As..." Save it to a file folder and then open the pdf document. Print the document and follow the instructions to complete the Spiritual Gifts Survey. Encourage everyone in your SAM to take advantage of this FREE offer from LifeWay. We encourage people to become leaders only in their areas of strong giftedness. If someone has their lowest score in 'Teaching,' DO NOT assign them as a Sunday School Teacher; they will struggle. Don't make someone with Evangelism as their lowest score the Outreach Leader of the class.

Never do ministry alone! Work to find others to partner with you and mentor them into leadership as best as you can. **Constantly watch and evaluate** others in your ministry as potential leaders. You need a constant flow of leaders. If you try to have two small groups with only one qualified leader, the other group will struggle and probably fail. As you grow, constantly teach others what you know. Maxwell says that the definition of leadership is: INFLUENCE, nothing more, nothing less. As you interact with single adults be watching for the positive influence they have with others. They are potential leaders.

NEVER compromise spiritual quality to get a *popular* person into leadership. A form to help you evaluate leaders is at Enclosure 7. Do a separate Profile on each possible leader. Make sure you know and abide by any Leadership Guidelines set by your church.

Develop a Leadership Team: As of this writing a search on the Internet returned 277 million results on the words, LEADERSHIP TEAM. Obviously, there is no shortage of ideas and recommendations surrounding the concept of forming a Leadership Team. But, in its basic form, a Leadership Team is not Rocket Science...it is more Common Sense.

If we start with God's idea we can find His recommendation in **Ecclesiastes 4:9-12**, *"Two are better than one, because they have a good return for their labor: If either of them falls down, one can help the other up. But pity anyone who falls and has no one to help them up. Also, if two lie down together, they will keep warm. But how can one keep warm alone?"*

That's it; *more than one* will always be better when you are doing ministry. In too many churches we have seen some leaders who insist that only *they* have the ability to lead a group, only to see the group dissolve when the leader falls or leaves for some reason. Your class should not flounder just because you are on vacation.

After reviewing many publications about *teams* and after years of experience leading as a team we have narrowed the basics of forming a team down to what we think is a manageable and doable level. Add your own research and experience to the format below. Teams, leading in all areas of ministry, will be the life-blood that moves your SAM forward.

FIRST: *Make Godly principles the backbone of every team.* Team members MUST be passionate and honest in their service to God and their expressions of Him. They must have active prayer lives and be in the process of learning and growing spiritually. They don't have to be *perfect* (none of us would qualify). But, set high standards. They need to know/admit that they are not where they need to be and be willing to work toward a closer relationship with God. When singles who attend the group see that the leaders *practice what they preach* they will know that your SAM has a solid spiritual foundation. This must be an *ongoing* process for leaders; not a one-time shot. Leaders who are not passionate about God can easily be seen as hypocrites if anything questionable creeps into their lives.

SECOND: *Work to know and understand single adults.* Even if you are single you will not automatically understand other singles, especially those in other categories apart from your life situation. Develop a heart for the singles in your target group. You cannot develop a plan to meet the various needs in their lives if you do not understand who they are and where they want to go in life. You have to spend quality time with singles, both in church and outside of church.

Establish an ongoing research of all resources you can find about the various categories of singles. Most important will be an understanding of who they are spiritually. You will want to equip and empower them but only at their level of spiritual development.

THIRD: *Learn the principles of team-building*. One principle is to communicate clearly with potential team members the **purpose and vision** of your SAM and the purpose of the ministry team you are recruiting them to be on. You must also find out what their dreams are and try to build teams with members who have common or similar dreams. Build trust among the team and help them see their part of the collective vision.

FOURTH: *Embrace variety and diversity when forming teams.* Meet often to ensure teams understand their responsibilities. Teach teams to be overt encouragers and good listeners to all of the diverse categories of singles and to keep leadership informed about the best practices for meeting their needs. Team members need to use appropriate resources to grow in their understanding of those to whom they minister. Be sure to listen to, evaluate and use the recommendations of team members.

Diversity in your ministry teams will also come from the presence of single leaders and married leaders. As we said at the beginning of this kit, marital status has little to do with the success of a team ministering to single adults. Remember, every married person was single before marriage. Passion and commitment to minister in the lives of others will always trump marital status. Whether single or married, always hold an unwavering standard of moral and relationship integrity. Moral failures of any leader will damage your SAM deeply.

Single leaders must live-out their relationships with Godly character. Married leaders must have and maintain faithfulness and integrity in their marriage. Whether single or married, DO NOT allow leaders to spend a lot of alone-time with members of the opposite sex, unless they are married to them. In **1 Thessalonians 5:22** the King James Version says to... "Abstain from any appearance of evil." The advantage of having leaders in solid Godly marriages is that it provides a good example for single adults to emulate.

Be aware that diversity brings different personalities together, which can sometimes cause a clash of ideas about the direction some endeavor should take. Conflicts among the team members can be minimized by fostering an atmosphere of prayer, love, and forgiveness.

FIFTH: *Form a 'Church Staff Coordination Team."* If your responsibilities are to lead the overall SAM you will need to interact with the Pastor and whatever church staff is in place. You need a team to take responsibility for staff coordination.

This team should also be diverse, knowledgeable about SAM and hold to the previous four essentials of team building. It is not essential but would be helpful if one or more on this team were professionals in their career fields, since they will be coordinating with professionals on the church staff. These team members need to get to know the church staff; their concerns, their vision for the church and be ready to show them how those in your SAM will partner with the staff in church and Kingdom growth. Encourage the Pastor to support you SAM vision and to consider single adults for other leadership roles in the church. Make sure your SAM leaders get to know the

Pastor's heart and commit to support and follow his leadership for the church.

If you are the Pastor, wanting to start a SAM, you need to look for a leader in the church that has a passion for God, for ministry, for church growth and for leading singles to deeper relationships with God. Make sure the leader is one that you have a good working relationship with; one that buys into YOU and the VISION for the church. Depending on your location in the country, approximately 50% of the adults in your area will be un-married. The *'Fields white unto harvest...'* contain a lot of single people. Be prepared to allocate at least some of the church's resources to support and grow a SAM.

SIXTH: *Team considerations for smaller churches.* In smaller churches the only staff member may be the Pastor. Even in small-church communities there will be a lot of single people; more than most Pastors think are there. Of course, YOU, the Pastor will be the starting point for developing a SAM...which may only start out with a small Bible Study.

We have seen some small churches where the starting point was just a week-night Bible Study at the Pastor's house, or at the home of a leader the Pastor recruited. Some later developed into Sunday School classes, although some had to meet off campus due to lack of space in the church building. We know of several that started as a Sunday morning class at a local restaurant.

Remember, though, even small SAMs will still follow the cycle of SAM displayed in Section 16 below, **Evaluating Your SAM.** The *ups and downs* displayed on the chart will be more pronounced in a smaller group. When starting with a small group, plan ahead to provide leaders for the future, when the growth in numbers and diversity will require new groups to form.

SAMPLE SAM LEADERSHIP/MINISTRY TEAMS: Below is a sample list of leadership teams and their intended functions. You may need some of these type teams or others that are not listed. Make sure that SAM leaders are ready to manage and evaluate the teams; ensuring they adhere to the Purpose and Vision.

    1. <u>Promotion and publicity team</u> - markets the single adult ministry and its activities in the church and community. Works closely with the Media Team.

    2. <u>Special events team</u> - envisions and coordinates retreats, conferences, seminars, and other special activities for single adults

    3. <u>Media team</u> - produces quarterly or monthly updates of activities and uses every available form of web site and social media outlets to inform single adults about the single adult ministry

    4. <u>Outdoor/outreach team</u> - connects single adults in relationships with God, self, and other through nature and recreation.

    5. <u>Friends ministry team</u> - helps single adults discover relationships with Christ and other Christian brothers and sisters

    6. <u>Community service projects team</u> - provides opportunities for single adults to give their time and service to others outside the church

    7. <u>Personal profile team</u> - involves single adults in identifying their spiritual gifts and personality styles and in assessing their experiences and interests to find their places in the Christian community

    8. <u>Small groups team</u> - develops small-groups learning experiences at a variety of times and in a variety of settings to disciple Christians and to create Christian community.

LEADERSHIP SCHOOL: We actually started an Annual Leadership School from the guidelines we developed. The effort you put into finding and growing leaders will be rewarded by ministry growth beyond your expectations. We charged $50 a year for materials. We met for two hours on a monthly basis to discuss the *homework* we had given them to read and analyze scripture, books, audio lessons and some interviews with business leaders we had assigned to them. We were gratified at the obvious growth of these leaders.

We went to leadership conferences and took our volunteer leaders with us. We encourage you to log onto www.johnmaxwell.com and find where the closest John Maxwell Leadership Conference will be and make plans to go.

List in the spaces below any potential leaders who have already come to mind. Begin praying for wisdom as you assess their potential to be leaders in your ministry. List them here and in Enclosure 6.

Name _____ **Phone** _____

Email _____

Name _____ **Phone** _____

Email _____

Name _____ **Phone** _____

Email _____

NOTES:

7. FACING LEADERSHIP CHALLENGES

Few things can discourage leaders more than challenges from within the church or in the ministry they lead. There are only two kinds of leaders; those who have faced challenges and those who WILL face challenges. Look at the great leaders highlighted in the Bible. ALL of them faced significant challenges in their service to God and His people.

In reality, challenges will come at some point in your ministry as you work to start and grow it. As we make suggestions we will assume that you are NOT the person causing the difficulty. There are several major areas in which single adult leaders are most often challenged. These are, *Spiritual, Moral, Personal* and *Philosophical*.

Spiritual challenges will come from those attracted to your ministry who come from a spiritual background different from yours, a different denomination or religion, or those whose spiritual foundation has been shaken by some event such as a divorce. Some will challenge the Bible's position on issues such as sexuality, divorce, forgiveness, tithing, etc. It is sad to have to admit that we church leaders over the last 50 years have allowed a *spiritual shallowness* to creep into our churches. Some single adults (and married people too) will reflect that same shallowness.

As you deal with spiritual challenges you must be well grounded in *who you are* spiritually. Be ready to share the basic truths about salvation and lead someone to accept the saving grace of Jesus. IF YOU CANNOT do that, you are not qualified to lead a SAM until you grow in that area of your life. Everything we do in SAM must point people to the Kingdom of Christ. Otherwise, what's the point?

Other leaders in your SAM, especially Bible Study Leaders, must be well grounded in God's Word and agree to be well prepared to lead each class. We who lead can't know everything but we can easily lose credibility when we make *assumptions* about the meaning of scripture instead of studying beforehand to better understand it. We've heard several leaders over the years teaching that *suicide* is the unpardonable sin! You can't find that anywhere in the Bible. Remind leaders that they are influencing people for the Kingdom. They must not take that responsibility lightly!

Moral challenges can destroy you and your SAM! Satan's first attack on leaders will come through the temptation toward immorality. Married leaders in SAM **must** have **solid** marriages to reduce mistrust between husband and wife as they minister to single people. Single leaders will be as challenged sexually as non-leaders and must commit to purity up front! Immoral temptations are everywhere! When it comes to the use of the Internet, **caution** must be the watch-word. **Porn** is just a *click* away anywhere on the Net. Recent reports of the increased viewing of porn by Christian leaders is very troubling. Remember, you can *never* hide completely the history files on your computer.

Only those who signed our Leadership Covenant were allowed to lead in our SAM. Single people who have suffered recent losses in their lives are more vulnerable to the need for love and affection and can easily choose an unhealthy relationship in an attempt to reduce the pain of their loss. Leaders in recovery-type support groups must have definite restrictions for themselves and be quick to caution those in the group against forming relationships with other group members.

Such relationships can quickly become immoral and delay the recovery process for years! When immorality is obvious, such as singles cohabitating, lovingly confront them with alternatives to their lifestyle. Be ready to Biblically support your position. Be slow to *kick them out*! Your SAM may be the only vehicle God is using to reach them.

Wise leaders will know their single adults well and will be cognizant of new people who may be *surfing* the group, looking only for dates, or the most serious *predators* who are out to use people for their own gratification. Be quick to confront them so that they know you are aware of their intentions. Be careful but be open to the working of the Holy Spirit in them. God can do miracles!

As your SAM grows you may have to face moral issues such as homosexuality, lesbianism, addictive behavior, child abuse, sexual abuse or other such issues. Unless you are experienced or trained to handle these issues you should quickly refer these people to those who can help them, such as your pastor or a professional counselor.

Confronting immorality in any circumstance is always difficult. But, if leaders are involved in some indiscretion, *you have no choice*! You cannot allow anyone else's poor choices to destroy ministry to those who need it so badly. If you must confront someone, it is best to take another leader with you. Be prayed up and prepared to extend love and grace, just as Jesus would do. But, be firm and remove the leader if necessary. DO NOT wait! It is tough but... *welcome to leadership*!

Personal challenges come more from personality differences and just plain selfishness within your SAM, particularly as it grows. If you are an insecure or a domineering leader and you hold leadership closely instead of sharing it with a team you are sure to clash with your other leaders. If your leaders are the same way they may want to build their own *kingdoms* within the ministry and may be resistant to change, growth or shared leadership. Avoid this by evaluating leaders well up front. We have seen too many promising SAMs decline or disappear because of personal differences among leaders.

Do not let Satan get that victory! Constantly remind leaders and all single adults *why* your SAM exists. Keep your Purpose, Vision and Goals Statements posted in all areas frequented by single adults. Review them often at leadership meetings. Remove people from leadership when necessary! Had you rather lose a leader or your whole SAM?

Philosophical challenges most often come from other areas of church leadership. These challenges are often bred in the saying, *"We've never done it that way before."* Single adult ministry will be new and suspect to some older church leaders. Some will assume that your SAM will be a *drain* on the church and the church is not equipped or funded to do the ministry. Most of us who are VMPs (very married people) got married very young and are still married. Therefore, many will not *welcome* divorced people and will be skeptical of older never-married single adults. In our area this attitude manifested itself through other churches referring over to us the single people who come to their churches! They would say, "You have a singles ministry and we don't, so we sent them to you." How sad, that these churches turn away potential church growth and ministry opportunities. Our prayer is that this kit will help some of those churches begin to minister in the lives of the single adults who come their way.

You can meet philosophical challenges by sharing the true statistics about single people and reminding church leaders that not only was Jesus single but He did His most notable ministry in the lives of single people, one on one. He also said in Matthew 25: 40, *"The King will reply, 'I tell you the truth, whatever you did for one of the least of these brothers of mine, you did for me."* Remind leaders of the contribution single adults are already making in the life of your church.

Lifestyle issues will become more of a challenge as society continues to change toward liberal thought. As we mentioned, most often the issue will be singles who decide to cohabitate before marriage or in lieu of marriage. Your leaders must be in agreement that a sexual relationship in cohabitation is unacceptable for Christians. **Train** your leaders to be proficient in explaining and teaching the Biblical principles involved. Be careful not to discourage those couples from attending your SAM; they will be more willing to change when they learn Christ's standards for relationships. Confront them only in love and build a relationship with them that gives you the *right* to be honest with them.

Another recent and *coming* challenge is those visiting or in your SAM who have chosen a homosexual lifestyle. Remember…same sex *tendencies* and *temptation* are NOT sins – homosexual **sexual** activity is the only same-sex sin listed in the Bible. Treat them like Jesus would…with love. But, teach the truth. When a gay man asked me (Max) if he could come to our Bible Study I answered this way; "If you want to come to explore spiritual issues, to learn more about God and Jesus and to determine if you want a personal relationship with Jesus…you are welcome. If you are coming to seek to justify your lifestyle or to seek out others who may be interested in your lifestyle…I will discourage you from coming. We are all about Jesus, His sacrifice for us and how our lives can be an example of His love for the world." He came a few times and then stopped. I counseled with him but he continued in his choice.

Other concerns can come in the form of single adults attracted to your ministry who are challenged mentally, socially or physically. Treat these people with love and understanding and get advice from church leadership and local professionals who deal often with such issues. Keep in mind, WWJD.

We have found that these *challenged* single adults can best be ministered to by caring leaders with high scores in the spiritual gifts of Mercy, Giving and Exhortation. Your concern will be that these people will create a negative atmosphere and render your SAM *unattractive* to visiting single adults. If your leaders will commit to helping the challenged singles *fit in,* they will begin to be less of a concern and visitors will see that yours is a group with compassion, which does not exclude people who are *different*.

Other than your pastor, ask who the local *Christian* counselors are and keep their information to share with those who need help beyond your capability. Ask the counselors if they accept the state-provided insurance for low-income earners, if applicable. List the professionals here and in Enclosure 6.

Name _____

Title _____

Phone _____ Accept Insurance? _____

Hourly Rate $_____

Name _____

Title _____

Phone _____ Accept Insurance? _____

Hourly Rate $_____

NOTES:

8. BUDGETING

Most beginning SAMs do not have an established budget. Some have to do fund-raising to get started. Work with your church leaders to stay within church guidelines but be consistent in your request for assistance from the church. Try to get at least SOMETHING in the budget, even if it is very small. With a line item for Single Adult Ministry listed in the Budget it becomes easier to increase it the next year.

Regardless of how you are funded **ALWAYS** be careful to track and account for all funds. Keep receipts and avoid using separate *personal* checking accounts. Work through the church financial office if at all possible. Always be ready to explain if anyone asks for the details of your use of funds at any Business/Budget Meeting in your church.

Coordinate with the person responsible for budgeting in your organization and ask to have a qualified single adult appointed to the Finance Committee. Be sure to select that person carefully so they will be a well-qualified member who will represent single adult issues and needs well.

NOTES:

9. DECIDING WHERE, HOW AND WHEN TO START

Some of the first questions most leaders ask is, "Where do I start? What format do I use? When choosing an Organizational Style, the basic considerations are: Purpose, Needs of Target Group, Church Strategy, Leadership Available, Organization of Sunday School and Resources available (space, budget, etc.

To help you assess the needs of your target group you can ask each person who is already there to complete an Information Survey, then ask every new person to do one. You will find the one we used at Enclosure 4. Copy the survey and modify it to fit your group. If you do a survey, be sure to actually *use the information*! We used our surveys to determine what seminars or classes needed to be offered and we only offered those classes. The classes were usually well attended. Form a team to compile and assess the surveys and to make recommendations as to actions you need to take.

Depending on your situation, your first group could be a Sunday School Class; the church already provides childcare at that time. If so, ask your Sunday School Director or Pastor or Education Staff member to help you get the space and order the curriculum. Ask them to recommend materials written specifically for single adults.

Or, your starting format may be an evening Bible Study, a Support Group (divorce recovery, grief recovery, etc), a Single Parent Group or something like a Sporting Event followed by a short Bible Study. Be open and creative but above all, make a commitment to START! Choose study materials to fit the needs of the group. ALWAYS use the Bible in some way as one of your study materials.

Remember, well-prepared leadership is the key to success. Be sure to provide a *space* that is as attractive as possible and one that has the facilities and materials to support the impact you want to make. Brainstorm with your leaders and write down what you think is the best format with which to start and who the other potential leaders are.

EVENTS can be great *entry points* into your ministry. Sporting events, pot lucks, picnics, restaurant trips, scavenger hunts, community work groups, etc., can all provide opportunities to meet new people and invite them to your SAM. When possible, collect their contact information and follow up personally. Have as many FREE events as possible.

SAM Format _____

Leader _____

SAM Format _____

Leader _____

In deciding WHEN to start, work with your church leadership to find the best start date, based on the projected Church Calendar. Then, check the Community Calendar to avoid local holidays, events and special community days that might draw people away from your Start Day.

For instance, during the Thanksgiving and Christmas holidays you would not want to start a weekly series on *Dating* or *How to Study the Bible* but it would be a perfect time to start a *Divorce* or *Grief Recovery* series, since such losses are felt more dramatically during the holidays.

Make sure your primary activity, maybe Sunday School, is well organized and supported. Have single people as greeters to welcome and sit with guests. If there are guests, everyone should wear nametags. *As a minimum,* leaders and greeters

should wear them. Start ONLY when you are ready-- not before!
Don't start if you won't or can't sustain the group.

NOTES:

HOLT & STEPHENS

10. ADVERTISING

People cannot come to something if they do not know it exists. Advertising, both inside and outside of your church is essential. Like most other advertising, word of mouth will always be the best. When peoples' needs are met they usually tell their friends and invite them to come see for themselves. The best person to reach a single adult is another single adult.

Those in your SAM are the best advertisement you can get. Encourage them to invite their friends to come with them. Organized 'Outreach or Visitation' can be a powerful tool to reach single people if those who do the visiting are single themselves. Be sure, within 48 hours of someone visiting your group, to contact the visitor to answer questions and invite them back. A personal visit is always best. If you wait a week the percentage of those returning is much smaller. Leaders can and should contact visitors but the best impact will always be by another single adult in the class contacting them. IMPORTANT: Males should contact males and females should contact females.

The first place to advertise is inside your church. Keep people informed as to your ministry goals and how the ministry fits into the overall Purpose of the church. Use your Worship Service Bulletins, website updates, newsletters, flyers, bulletin boards, announcements, facebook posts, twitter tweets or whatever the next social media outlet happens to be. Here is a sample announcement.

NEW SUNDAY SCHOOL CLASS FOR SINGLE ADULTS!
Anywhere Baptist Church is beginning a new Sunday School class, especially for all Single Adults over 30. The new class will be start on October 5th at 9:30 a.m. in room 105. John & Lisa Wilson, 931-648-8031, will be the teachers. Their email is

jlwilson@anywhereemail.com. Contact them or the Sunday School Director for more details. Please invite all of the single adults you know to help start this new class.

Contact your church's webmaster to get space on the church web site for SAM information and to get SAM events listed on the site calendar. IMPORTANT: Keep web site information *current*! Out-of-date information is an indicator that you aren't interested in excellence in your ministry. Twitter, facebook and other such outlets are great media tools to reach singles, especially younger singles. Use them!

The other obvious place to advertise is outside the church. We developed a folding business card with our logo, a map to the church and a ministry summary. It was very useful both inside and outside the church. We left the cards with tips at restaurants (leave GOOD tips!) and any other location we happened to frequent.

If you want to reach **young** adults it is hard to beat Social Media. We still used flyers in commercial locations that allowed them to be posted. Flyers in larger grocery stores, laundry mats and at Mall locations will reach a diversity of ages. To reach single parents, flyers can go to Day Care locations. To reach the over 35 group, do flyers in Laundry Mats.

Another useful tool is a News Release, which provides information about an event we have scheduled. We emailed News Releases to 11 different media organizations, requesting that they do a Public Service Announcement. The FCC requires that all radio stations and newspapers do a certain number of free announcements for the good of the public. These may not run at the exact times you want but they are FREE! We used them extensively. Be sure to send to secular media as well as Christian media. Below is a sample of the News Release we used.

NEWS RELEASE   *September 15, 2015*
For Immediate Release
Hilldale Baptist Church
For information Contact Max Holt
2001 Madison St
Clarksville, TN 37010
931-648-8031

NEW SINGLE ADULT GROUP STARTING

Hilldale Baptist Church, 2001 Madison Street near the Carmike 8 Theaters, is beginning its first group especially for single people over 30, starting on Sunday, October 5th. The group will meet every Sunday at 9:30 a.m. in the main church building. Childcare is provided. Come and make some new friends in a caring environment. Explore who you are spiritually and see what the Bible has to say about real answers to life's real questions. For more information call Max at 931-648-8031 or go to www.hilldale.org (click on Singles.)

It is important that you get to know the media people in your area. Go to the newspapers and the radio stations as your time allows and get to know the News Directors. Write or email them to explain what your organization is all about. You may be thinking that singles, especially young singles, don't read the newspaper. Generally, that's true. BUT...their parents and grandparents DO. They can often influence young singles in their families to begin attending church.

We listened to a local radio talk show for a few days, then called the News Director and asked to be on the show to discuss single adults. The Director was amazed to learn the statistics on singleness and not only agreed but invited us back several times to discuss details. For several years we had an open invitation to drop in anytime and they would put us on the air. List the media outlets below which reach into your area. Begin to contact and visit them, after you have decided on a plan to implement your ministry. List here and in Enclosure 6.

Media _____

Phone_____

Email_____

News Director _____

Call Letters (if applicable) _____

Radio frequency _____

Media _____

Phone_____

Email_____

News Director

_____

Call Letters (if applicable) _____

Radio frequency _____

Media _____

Phone_____

Email_____

News Director _____

Call Letters (if applicable) _____

Radio frequency _____

Media _____

Phone_____

Email_____

News Director _____

Call Letters (if applicable) _____

Radio frequency _____

Media _____

Phone_____

Email_____

HOLT & STEPHENS

News Director _____

Call Letters (if applicable) _____

Radio frequency _____

Media _____

Phone_____

Email_____

News Director _____

Call Letters (if applicable) _____

Radio frequency _____

NOTES:

11. START DAY!

Start Day will be a big day for your new ministry. Make it a big deal! Meet with leaders to pray together before the event begins. Our Prayer Team met EVERY Sunday before the first class began. Prepare properly and advertise well in advance. Do everything with excellence. Make sure everyone on your Leadership Team is involved. Plan the setup, decorating, food, Bible Study and other activities to start and end on time.

Prepare some information flyers or cards about your SAM to give to every guest. We used an inexpensive large envelop filled with flyers, cards, church information, and a ticket for one free Wednesday night church meal. Your team will need to do a follow-up assessment of how it went and be prepared to make changes as necessary. **Be sure** to have a plan to follow up on the guests who visited that day. They are the key to near-term growth of your SAM.

Sunday School, or whatever you call your primary Sunday Morning activity, seems to be the best vehicle to facilitate starting a new Single Adult Ministry. It will usually produce the largest crowd and Child Care is usually already provided.

Once again, the leader of that class MUST be a willing, excited, well-prepared leader. The class doesn't need a preacher; they need a *teacher/facilitator* who will lead them into personal discovery of Biblical truth. Small group discussion and interaction will always be welcome. The old, *sit in rows, lecture from the podium* method will not cut it with single adults.

CAUTION: Do NOT ask new members or guests to **read** from the Bible or other material, or to **pray** or ask them questions directly, which require exact spiritual answers. You run the risk of embarrassing them. Opinion questions are great as long as you do not judge their answers directly.

List in the spaces below those who will be involved in leading various aspects of your start day. Also put them on the Consolidated List at Enclosure 6.

Teacher/Leader _____

Phone _____

Email _____

Setup _____

Phone _____

Email _____

Snacks/Food _____

Phone _____

Email _____

Greeters _____

Phone _____

Email _____

Follow up _____

Phone _____ _

Email _____

NOTES:

12. SPECIAL NEEDS

It is important to remember that leaders of special targeted ministries must be *peers* of those who will attend. I (Max) am a VMP (Very Married Person) so I'm not qualified to lead Divorce Recovery or Single Parenting. Doug and Sara Stephens were both previously divorced and got married after meeting in our singles ministry. They ARE qualified to lead such ministries. Leaders must have *been there, done that, made it through* before they can lead others through. Be sure to keep recovery-type classes separate from Bible Study or other activities. Otherwise, your whole ministry will start to reflect recovery issues and only those in need will come.

A majority of single adults *are not* dealing with these issues and just need a place to grow spiritually without having to deal with non-relevant issues. Other needs will be met by providing future training or classes in Lifestyle Issues. Remember; be quick to refer people with challenging issues, outside your capabilities, to the Pastor or another professional.

NOTES:

13. DOCUMENTING YOUR MINISTRY

It will be very important that you document well all activities of your ministry. Keep good files and records. During the 15 years that we led our SAM we knew how many had been saved & baptized, average attendance in Sunday School, number married, number who went through pre-marriage counseling, number that we trained and who went to teach in other classes in the church, the number of singles in the choir & orchestra, the number on committees, the number who lead other ministries during the week, the number who went through Leadership School, the number trained as Ministry Leaders through the school, the number of Ministry Teams formed and the ministries they accomplished and other information which highlighted the success of our ministry. We also reported census information about the total number of single adults in our ministry area, which had not yet been reached.

We summarized the information in an Annual Single Adult Ministry Report, done 2 months before Budget Time. There was a paragraph listing our goals for the next year. We set a goal for mentoring people to *leave* our ministry and become leaders in other classes in the church. It happens every year anyway, so we set that as a goal! We provided copies to the Pastor, Deacons and Budget Committee. The first time we did the report, the Budget Committee doubled our budget! They figured we needed more money to keep doing all we were doing and to reach the large number of single adults here. A format of our Single Adult Ministry Report is attached as ENCLOSURE 5.

NOTES:

14. CREATIVE IDEAS

Have regular brainstorming sessions with your leaders and all others willing to give input on creative ways to grow your SAM. Tailor the ideas to your community and your group. One example in Clarksville, TN was the annual Riverfest Celebration. We often rented booth space along the river and provided free bottled water with our logo pasted on the side. We also gave out ministry information and FREE meal tickets for our church's Wednesday night dinner. Monthly, the kitchen staff would report the number of tickets used and the Budget Office would charge the expense to our budget. Ask new people to help brainstorm new ideas, because they have *new eyes* and can see things others have long ago overlooked.

When implementing activities associated with these great ideas be sure to consider all groups within your ministry. Everyone will appreciate low cost events; especially lower income and single parents. If possible, plan events when childcare is already available. Otherwise, be sure to arrange for childcare when needed. Check the church calendar to make sure your event does not conflict with another scheduled event, which might occupy space, or resources you will need.

NOTES:

15. INVOLVING SINGLE ADULTS IN THE CHURCH

There is a place for everyone to serve in the church. The most obvious places are Choir, Children/Preschool Worker, Nursery, Door Greeters, Ushers or maybe Praise Team and Drama. Single adults will feel more a part of the church family if they get involved in the ministries of the church.

Work with church leaders to recommend single adults for leadership and committee positions. Use the list of ministries in Section 18 below to help single adults get involved. Talk to the Chairman of the Nominating Committee, or whoever recruits committees in your church, and ask him/her to look for committee positions for single adults. Learn the skills and talents of your single adults and recommend specific names for known positions, which are open. Most importantly, ASK single adults where they would like to serve in the church. Work to help them serve in those areas. List the people responsible for involving others in such areas.

Name _____ Phone _____

Email _____

Name _____ Phone _____

Email _____

Name _____ Phone _____

Email _____

NOTES:

HOLT & STEPHENS

16. EVALUATE YOUR SAM

Self-evaluation is always a difficult thing. All of us like to think that we are already doing the BEST job possible. But, as the saying goes, *"There is always room for improvement."* In Jim Collins' well-known business book, **Good to Great**, he explores what it takes for businesses to go from being a GOOD business to being a GREAT business. He said something in his book that really stood out. He said: "The enemy of Great is.....Good." He went on to say that all too often the leaders of organizations will **settle** for being *good* because there is a lot of work required to become *great*.

John Maxwell put it this way: "The biggest barrier to tomorrow's success is... today's success." We once heard a leader say: "Don't try to grow a great SAM. Concentrate on growing great people and let *them* grow a great SAM." We agree. As you evaluate every aspect of your ministry be sure you are analyzing the methods you are using in your training/teaching/leading/influencing of the singles who attend. Your SAM may be *good* but we pray that you will sense God's leadership to make it a *great* SAM.

Before you can properly evaluate your SAM you need to understand the NORMAL LIFE CYCLE of a Healthy SAM. The following chart illustrates the growth cycle that most SAMs experience. The explanation of the chart follows it.

SAM GROWTH CHART

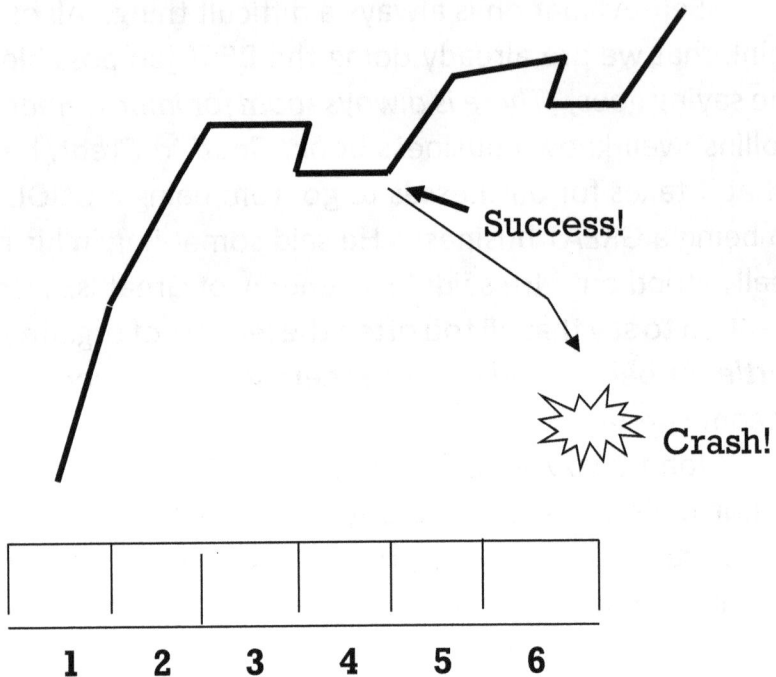

The numbers across the bottom represent 'Periods of Time.' For our SAM the first 3 periods were years. The following periods were shorter. The vertical direction on the chart represents the 'Growth in Attendance.' When we 'formalized' the SAM at Hilldale Baptist there were 32 singles and leaders in attendance the first day. The first year we grew by 62.5%...to 52 in regular attendance.

The second year the growth was 38.5%...to 72 in average attendance. But, the third year the growth in 'average attendance' went from 72 to 73...a whopping 1.4%!! At the beginning of the 4th year, the average attendance soon dropped to 65; an 11% decrease! WHAT HAPPENED?! That's what we wanted to know. What seemed like a failure stopped us in our tracks. So, we put on our analyst hats and looked at every detail of our SAM.

Here's what we discovered. During the first 2 years there was a lot of excitement among area singles, over the creation of a special ministry for them. Many regular attendees began to grow spiritually and began exercising leadership in the group. Also, due in part to our excellent relationship training, many quality relationships formed in the group. Near the end of the second year, two important things began to happen: First, those leaders who were growing began to commit to Sunday-Morning leadership and ministry in the church and began leaving the Bible Study classes to teach and lead in other areas of the church. That's a good thing! Also, those couples who had been forming relationships started getting married and moving into the Married Ministry of the church. THAT, is also a good thing!

Finally, many young adults and young soldiers from Fort Campbell had been attracted to the group. The transient nature of these groups had caused continuous turn-over in that demographic. Looking at the **numbers** we discovered that we had actually had 27 new singles join and regularly attend the group that third year...BUT...26 others had left the group for the *good* reasons just described.

Notice on the chart that there is both a drop in attendance and a line with a backward slope to it. The backward slope indicates a decrease in the number and experience of our leadership base. Without some of the experienced leaders/teachers we had had for the first 2 years we lost some of our momentum.

Look at that first cycle: Up, up, level, down and backward. THAT, is the normal cycle of a *healthy* SAM. So, we refined and increased out outreach efforts. We began aggressive efforts at training more leaders, which led to a *formal* Leadership School being developed.

Well into the 4th year we began to see the changes pay off, with growth in all areas. We discovered that if overall church growth is...say...10%, the SAM has to grow at a rate of about 20%, just to keep up. We also discovered that we could not totally eliminate the DOWN/BACKWARD slope on the chart; we could just *minimize* its impact on the ministry. The SUCCESS point indicated on the chart is the point at which we **'got it.'** We understood what it would take to revitalize our SAM and begin growing again.

HOWEVER, ...we have seen too many church leaders look at the **numbers** at that point and decide that, *"This singles thing isn't working, so let's pull the plug."* So, they decide to defund it and maybe reassign leaders and the SAM goes down that *crash & burn* line on the chart. Sadly, even some large churches have misunderstood the *numbers* and have abandoned their efforts to reach approximately 50% of the adult population in their areas. Very sad!

However, our SAM rebounded and continued growing. There were several years that there were 30 or more singles who were saved and baptized as they came into the group. During our ministry there were 352 singles married out of our group; still with overall divorce rates over 70% LOWER than the national average.

So, as you evaluate, keep the Growth Chart in mind. You must be ready to START what needs to be started and (the hard part) you must STOP what needs to be stopped. Reportedly there is an old Indian saying, which goes like this, *"When you discover you are riding a dead horse, the best thing to do is to dismount!"* Be careful not to let a class or ministry deteriorate into a 'dead' activity. Constantly watch and listen so you can accurately evaluate how your SAM is doing.

Keep your leaders involved in the process so they will be open to changes necessary to keep the ministry fresh. As your SAM grows you will need to adjust your organization. Let teachers know early on that an indication of their success will be the necessity to CREATE new classes or ministries. Use the word, **CREATE.** **NEVER** use the word **SPLIT** when you start new groups/classes.

One idea for starting a new class is to routinely divide a large class into small discussion groups during the regular Bible Study time. Some would call this concept the MASTER-TEACHER concept, where a primary teacher begins the class with a summary Bible Study of the lesson, followed by small well-led groups that would discuss the material, including the application of the lesson to their lives.

The groups should be divided based on common identification, i.e., age, gender, life-situation, etc. The small group leaders should be those who are ready to lead a class on their own. After several weeks one or more of the small groups can do their small-group time in another room. Soon, that group can just start meeting first in the room and be designated as a separate class.

Another idea for creating a new class is to **first** get the leader, and then get 2 or 3 'seed' people from other classes to help the leader start. Concentrate on inviting new people from outside of your SAM. Some in the other classes will eventually gravitate to the new class if it is in their age range. If you state this plan up front, your leaders will less prone to become possessive when their class grows large. Recognize leaders publicly when they help *birth* a new class.

Remember, the larger the class, the less discussion, the less interaction and the less learning will take place. To meet the *need* for a large group atmosphere you can have an opening praise time or summary Bible Study with everyone together, and then break into classes.

CAUTION: Large group times can be time-wasters unless they are well led, creative and done with excellence. An indication that your large group time is failing will be the number of single adults who arrive late so they will be in time for the small group time only. As you build a leadership team let them be the evaluators of the atmosphere you create. Be sure to listen to them!

Another caution: Some leaders will become territorial, meaning that they don't want to give up part of their class even though starting a new group is part of a healthy growth plan for any SAM. Work with that leader; revisit the SAM Purpose and Vision. If the leader refuses to be part of the SAM growth you may have to remove the leader...with love and compassion. You cannot allow a reluctant leader to hinder the growth of your SAM, which will hinder the growth of the Kingdom and, more importantly, hinder some single from coming to Christ.

Final caution: Make sure *your own* leadership is done with excellence before you challenge another's leadership.

NOTES:

17. EMPOWERING SINGLE ADULTS

Another appropriate title for this section would be, "Giving The Ministry Away," because that's what *empowerment* is all about; allowing singles to have authority in determining the direction of your SAM.

For our purposes the word **empowering** will mean *enabling* single adults to be *real* ministers through improving their capabilities and by giving *permission* for them to take ownership of your SAM. Many leaders have asked us how to sustain or grow their SAM. Truthfully, growth really begins when you *give your ministry away*; that is, when you give ownership of the success of the ministry to others. At a John Maxwell conference, I heard him say: "There are few limits on growth if you don't care who gets the credit." It is hard for some leaders to stay in the background and let single people reach and minister to each other. We pray that you are a leader who can do that!

Empowering single adults to do ministry is more than just saying it is OK for them to lead ministry. It is the ACT of teaching single adults the importance of *them doing* ministry in the lives of others. It involves a *plan* to teach them HOW to do ministry....together, in teams.

Two excellent books on the subject are now out of print but are available on some used books sites. They are; "Giving the Ministry Away" by Hershey and "Start A Revolution" by Felts. An Internet search will find other writings that address the subject from many points of view.

Here are some of the main points we concentrated on when we taught EMPOWERMENT to our single adults.

FIRST, we assembled everyone in our SAM who would agree to consider being on a leadership team or a ministry team. We created a *seminar setting* and scheduled them to meet with us every week. Our training ended up being ten weeks long. We wanted them to understand and admit WHO they were and WHERE they were, spiritually and personally. We have already discussed the importance of knowing your spiritual gifts. We also wanted them to understand the different personalities they would encounter among other singles. So we asked ALL singles and leaders in our SAM to complete a Personality Profile and to take a Spiritual Gifts Survey, if they hadn't taken one in the previous year.

We gave you the link to the Spiritual Gifts Survey, free from LifeWay. A search for *Personality Profile* on the Internet will result in many different ones available, for free. Use one that includes an explanation of the various personalities. Use the same one for everybody. Everyone did the Personality and Gifts assessments during our first session.

It was important for them to know that EVERYONE would get a score in ALL of the spiritual gifts listed in the Survey. Most had the idea that they had ONLY ONE spiritual gift. The survey showed a score in all gifts but also revealed which gifts God had strengthened in the lives. We made photo copies of their summary sheets, showing the scores in all of the Ministry Gifts. We would use these later to select singles to be on various ministry teams.

SECOND, we concentrated on the importance of having and displaying Godly character. We used men like King David and The Apostle Paul as Biblical examples of character. We brainstormed the various ways each of them could begin to grow deeper spiritually. Together we researched the resources that were available to help each of us begin a Personal Growth Plan.

We encouraged mentoring relationships in the group, who would also act as accountability partners. We discussed what a display of Godly character would look like at their jobs and other places they go in the community. We asked everyone in the seminar to agree to and sign the Leadership Covenant, at Enclosure 3. There were only a few who would not sign. They could stay in the training but would not be assigned a leadership position.

THIRD, we helped them (and us) take a fresh look at how we **needed** to minister to the world around us, rather than how we had *always done it.* One example was that traditionally, people in need of food would have to come to the church and ask for help. One of our singles came up with the idea to take food to the homes of those in need. Eventually the result was a significant food and toy ministry at Christmas to single parents in the area, where our singles delivered it to their homes. As our ministry teams formed we wanted them to take the initiative to design ministries they thought were appropriate.

We talked a lot about team dynamics and the importance of the teams to all-inclusive and to work together at whatever ministry they chose, giving it their concerted effort to ensure the ministry was successful.

FOURTH, we got down to the details of what ministries needed to be done and which singles in the group were best gifted to accomplish the various ministries. In some cases, we would assign a specific ministry that we knew was important enough to implement right away.

We reviewed the Purpose and Vision of our church and SAM and helped the teams clarify and narrow the purpose and vision of their ministry team. We reminded them that our ministry teams would be *fluid*, in that they would not last *forever*. Each team would have a specific ministry, some of which could be accomplished quickly.

Our Habitat For Humanity Team worked on houses under the guidance of the local Habitat House Office. It was a summertime ministry which ended when the houses were complete. Some teams would have long-term goals, such as the Church Staff Coordination Team. Teams accomplishing a short-term ministry would be assigned another one or would be integrated into other teams.

FIFTH, we got down to the details of defining the scope and membership of each ministry team and had them gather as teams to define their plan for accomplishing their ministry. This involved them brainstorming the details of what was needed to get the ministry started. They compiled lists of materials needed, estimated budget money needed, coordination needed, any permissions or permits that would be needed, etc. They defined the VISION of what they expected IF the accomplished their ministry. We cautioned our teams to realize that sometimes things would not go as planned and they would have to display innovative flexibility and keep their eyes on the vision of the ministry. We spent time with those team members who were considered *skilled* in areas needed for the team and with those who eventually exercised leadership in crucial areas of their ministry. We wanted these singles to realize the importance of mentoring others to take their place if they left or had to be absent for a period of time.

The whole Empowerment process took about ten weeks. It was so successful that we quickly started another seminar for others who had not participated in the first one. The results of the training were two-fold. First, excitement and spiritual growth was evident in our SAM as singles saw first-hand the results of their ministry efforts—many people were helped in many ways. Second, the overall excitement attracted new singles to the group and our attendance grew at a faster pace than before. Giving the ministry away to your singles will always reap spiritual dividends.

We feel strongly that a Team of two people should lead the Empowerment Seminar; it illustrates the *team* concept you are teaching. You need to teach it with creativity and excitement. After you complete the training it will be **very important** that you monitor your single adults' ministry teams, ensuring they accomplish their purpose. See Section 18 at the end of this kit for ministry team ideas.

One final note about spiritual gifts; do your best to keep singles in their areas of strong giftedness. For example, if my strongest gift is Teaching and my weakest is Mercy it would make sense to mentor me to teach a Bible Study Class rather than assign me to lead a Nursing Home Ministry. You may want to display copies of their Spiritual Gifts Survey summary sheet in your classrooms. That way, singles who have an idea for a ministry team can find others with similar gifts to partner with them. This method worked very well for us!

NOTES:

HOLT & STEPHENS

18. MEANINGFUL MINISTRIES

Ministries provide opportunities for single adults to give of themselves to others. Jesus said that He came to *serve*, not to be served. It is only through serving that we can properly express what God has done for us. Lead single adults to form Ministry Teams focused on helping and making a difference in the lives of others. In the spaces below list the ministry opportunities inside the church (all of the groups with opportunities to serve; choir, nursery, children's classes, ushers, van driver, etc) and outside the church (Habitat House, Food Kitchens, Disaster Relief, Christmas Toys, etc.)

Encourage single adults to view their world and to look for new ministries they feel are needed. List the point of contact for each Ministry and coordinate with them to determine the requirements for people to participate in that Ministry.

Ministry _____

Contact _____

Phone _____

Email _____

Description

_____

Ministry _____

Contact _____

HOLT & STEPHENS

Phone _____

Email _____

Description

_____

Ministry _____

Contact _____

Phone _____

Email _____

Description

_____

Ministry _____

Contact _____

Phone _____

Email _____

Description

_____

Ministry _____

Contact _____

Phone _____

Email _____

Description

_____

Ministry _____

Contact _____

Phone _____

Email _____

Description

_____

Ministry _____

Contact _____

Phone _____

Email _____

Description

_____

HOLT & STEPHENS

Ministry _____

Contact _____

Phone _____

Email _____

Description
_____

Ministry _____

Contact _____

Phone _____

Email _____

Description
_____

Ministry _____

Contact _____

Phone _____

Email _____

Description

_____

Ministry _____

Contact _____

Phone _____

Email _____

Description

_____

Ministry _____

Contact _____

Phone _____

Email _____

Description

_____

NOTES:

HOLT & STEPHENS

19. OTHER SINGLE ADULT MINISTRY RESOURCES

Books/Bible Studies/Leadership Materials
NOTE: We have NOT personally reviewed all of the web sites and resources listed below. Be aware that the Internet is a changing resource and can be manipulated by others for illicit purposes, including the unauthorized download of viruses to your computer. Use caution when searching or visiting web sites, even the ones listed as CHRISTIAN. There is always a possibility that information will be corrupted or misused in some way.

The following list was graciously provided to us by Kris Swiatocho, Director of The Singles Network Ministries, the largest resource for pastors and leaders who minister to single adults. Kris can be reached at Kris@thesinglesnetwork.org or on the web at http://www.thesinglesnetwork.org. We invite you to visit her site for the largest list of single adult ministry resources available anywhere and to see a schedule of appropriate events designed for Single Adults and Leaders.

Census Information.
Visit, http://2010.census.gov. This is a somewhat complicated site. One way to start is to click on the blue bar labeled (QuickFacts), then click on your state. From there just explore until you find what you are looking for. *Singles info for your state can be found at* http://www.census.gov/prod/cen2010/briefs/c2010br-14.pdf Scroll several pages down to find the Data listed by State. *Info on national statistics about marital status:* (divorced, never-married, widowed, etc.) www.census.gov/population/socdemo/hh-fam/p20-537/2000/tabA1.pdf

Building Leaders for your Singles Ministry
• Outflow by Steve Sjogren
• Why Men Hate Going to Church by David Murrow
• Reaching Boomers and Beyond by Amy Hanson• Generation Ex-Christian: Why Young Adults Are Leaving the Faith. . .and How to Bring Them Back by Drew Dyck
• How to Start a Single Mom's Ministry Kit by Jennifer Maggio
• College Ministry from Scratch by Chuck Bomar
• The Ways of the Alongsider by the Navigators
• Correspondence College Course on How to Start Singles Ministry by Dennis Franck
• Troublesome Bible Passages by David Watson (leaders guide)
• Ten Stupid Things That Keep Churches from Growing by Geoff Surratt
• Reaching Single Adults by Dennis Franck
• Developing a Single Adult Ministry by Dennis Franck
• Growing Your Single Adult Ministry: 60 Leaders Tell You How, compiled by Jerry Jones, editor of SAM Journal
• The Idea Catalog for Single Adult Ministries, compiled by Jerry Jones, editor of Single Adult Ministries Journal
• Creative Weekends: 23 1/2 Ready-To-Use Events for Single Adult Ministry by Paul Petersen
• Giving the Ministry Away: Empowering Single Adults for Effective Leadership by Terry Hershey
• Building Your Leadership Team: 200 Practical Ideas for Single Adult Ministry by Ed Weising
• Jesus on Leadership: Becoming a Servant Leader by C. Gene Wilkes
• Developing a Divorce Recovery Ministry by Bill Flanagan
• Single and Gifted by Brown
• Baker Handbook of Single Adult Ministry by Douglas L. Fagerstrom

• Spiritual Leadership by Henry and Richard Blackaby
• John C. Maxwell- Any book is great for leaders.
• Thirsty People: Developing a Step-family ministry in your church by Jeff and Judy Parziale
• Understanding and Ministering to Step-families (CD's) by Ron Deal
• Comforting the Bereaved: For Pastors and Others Who Minister by Warren W. Wiersbe, David W. Wiersbe
• Pastoral Care for Singles Parents plus many more books on grief by Harold Ivan Smith
• More than "I do", A Pastor's Resource book for Pre-Marital Counseling by Harold Ivan Smith
• Grief Care Kit for Pastors/Churches by Harold Ivan Smith
• Pre-marriage/Relationship Building Kit by Within Reach
• Discovering Intimacy: Experiencing Great Commandment Love in Single Adult Relationships:
   Leader's Guide by David Ferguson (workbook, video, and CD)

Bible Study/Sunday School Curriculum/Small Group
• Jesus, Single Like Me by Kris Swiatocho, includes leadership guide and study questions.
• Navpress Resource list [doc]
• Experiencing God for Young Adults by Henry Blackaby
• Bible Studies for Life for Young Adults (Lifeway)
• 20/30 Bible Study for Young Adults Faith by Clifton Guthrie and Barbara K Mittman
• Living Single by Tony Evans
• When I Became a Man by James Daughtry
• Not a Fan by Kyle Idleman
• Follow Me by David Platt
• 1 is a Whole Number by Robert Tauber
• Singles & Relationships by Kris Swiatocho, Dick Purnell (downloadable small group outline)

- Lies Women Believe by Nancy DeMoss
- Before You Plan Your Wedding, Plan Your Marriage by Dr. Greg an Erin Smalley
- Any study by Beth Moore
- Having a Mary Spirit by Joanna Weaver
- He Speaks to Me by Priscilla Shirer
- Crazy Love by Francis Chen (DVD's available)
- From the Manger to the Cross, The Single Women in Jesus's Life by Kris Swiatocho
- Anything by Tommy Nelson (specific Songs of Solomon)
- The Parable of Jesus Serendipity Bible Study
- Walk on Water by John Ortberg
- Several Studies by Andy Stanley
- Thirsty Thursday's by Marcus King
- Lessons in Christian Singleness by Ernest Jefferson
- Single Identity by Ernest Jefferson
- Being Single and the Spiritual Quest by Lifeway
- Leading from your Strengths by John Trent, Rodney Cox
- Lady In Waiting by Debbie Jones, Jackie Kendall (Journal/ Study Guide Available)
- Dating with Pure Passion by Rob Eagar (DVD/Study Kit available)
- Divorce Care Bible Study
- Divorce Care for Kids Bible Study

Bible Study/Personal Devotion
- Insightful Tips for the Unique Mature Single By Andrea Best
- Love Does by Bob Goff
- Singles & Relationships by Kris Swiatocho and Dick Purnell
- Jesus, Single Like Me by Kris Swiatocho, includes leadership guide and study questions.
- 1 is a Whole Number by Robert Tauber
- Random Thoughts: Get Real with God, Others, and Yourself:

A Devotional for Young Adults by Steve Russo
• Single Supplement by Margaret Ann Howie
• From the Manger to the Cross, The Single Women in Jesus's Life by Kris Swiatocho
• After Prayer by Dr. Moses Caesar
• The Circle Maker by Mark Batterson
• When God doesn't Answer Your Prayer by Jerry Sittser
• How Jesus Became Christian by Barrie Wilson
• The Allure of Hope by Jan Meyers
• Crazy Love by Francis Chan (book/DVD)
• Women Home Alone by Patrician Houck Sprinkle
• Learning to Love: Relationships Series by Lifeway
• One Like Jesus by Debra Farrington
• Single to God: Personal Prayers by Single Adults Through Everyday Life by Douglas L. Fagerstrom
• Single Purpose: A Devotion for Singles by H. Norman Wright
• The Single Journey by Peter Nadeau
• Sacred Rhythms by Ruth Haley Barton
• 5 Languages of Apology by Gary Chapman
• Latte for One and Loving It by Tosha Williams, Melanie Dobson
• Joyfully Single in a Couples World by Harold Sala
• A Singular Devotion: 366 Portraits of Singles Who Have Changed the World by Harold Ivan Smith
• Single to God: 100 Personal Prayers by Single Adults by Harold Ivan Smith
• They Were Single Too: 8 Biblical Role Models by David Hoffeditz

Relationships (General)
• 5 Love Languages for Singles by Gary Chapmen
• Straight Talk to Christian Singles by Kevin Paterson
• Safe People by Townsend and Cloud

• Singles and Lonely: Finding the Intimacy You Desire by Jayne V. Clark
• Safe People by Dr. Henry Club and Dr. John Townsend
• Lady In Waiting by Debbie Jones, Jackie Kendall (Journal/ Study Guide Available)
• You and Your Parents: Strategies to Building and Adult Relationship by Harold Ivan Smith

Relationships (Romantic/Dating)
• Hope for New Relationships by Dr. Dennis Henderson
• Insightful Tips For The Unique, Mature Single by Andrea Best
• Let's Talk About Sex and Relationships by Tania Vaughn
• How to Marry Contentment and Singleness by Bill D. Thrasher
• True Love Dates by Debra Fileta
• 10 Great Dates Before You Say "I Do" by David Arp
• The Waiting Room by TC Spellen
• Single, Ready and Waiting by Tanika Chambers
• 101 Questions to Ask before you get Engaged by H. Norman Wright
• Matched for Marriage, Meant for Life by Nate Stevens
• We're Just Friends and Other Dating Lies by Pastor Chuck Milian
• Unlocked: Breaking the Relationship Code by Conway and Jada Edwards
• Woman Don't Be Stupid by James Armato
• Undressed; The Naked Truth about Dating by Jason Illian
• Men Like Waffles..Women Like Spaghetti book and study guide by Bill & Pam Farell
• Love, Sex and Lasting Relationships by Chip Ingram
• 51 Good Things to Do until the Right one Comes Along by Harold Ivan Smith
• 10 Commandments of Dating by Ben Adams & Dr. Sam Young

- Love and Respect by Emerson Eggerichs and Thomas Nelson
- Rating Your Dating While You are Waiting by Ed Young, Jr.
- Men Like Waffles..Women Like Spaghetti book and study guide by Bill & Pam Farell
- Finding A Lasting Love by Dick Purnell
- Relationship Regret by Dick Purnell
- How to get a date worth keeping by Henry Cloud
- What to Do Until Loves Finds You by Michelle McKinney Hammond
- The UnGuide to Dating by Camerin Courtney, Todd Hertz
- Dating with Pure Passion by Rob Eagar (DVD/Study Kit available)
- Should I Get Married by M. Blaine Smith
- Secrets of an Irresistible Woman by Michelle McKinney Hammond
- Saving Your Marriage Before It Starts by Dr. Les and Leslie Parrott
- Knight in Shining Armor by PB Wilson
- A Good Man is Hard to Find by Jo Lynne Pool
- Finding the Love of Your Life by Neil Clark Warren
- Choosing God's Best by Dr. Don Raunikar
- Settling for Less Than God's Best by Elsa Kok
- Discovering Intimacy: Experiencing Great Commandment Love in Single Adult Relationships:
    Leader's Guide by David Ferguson (workbook, video, and CD)
- Reconcilable Differences by Jim Talley, Leslie H. Stobbe
- Smart Love: A Field Guide for Single Adults by Nancy L. Van Pelt
- Are We Compatible? by C. E. Rollins
- Any book by Les and Leslie Parrott
- Getting Along with People You Love: Building and Maintaining Healthy Relationships by Marilyn Moravec
- What You Need to Know Before You Fall in Love by David

Nicholson
• The Secret of Loving by Josh McDowell
• Boundaries in Dating by Henry Cloud, John Townsend
• Fit to Be Tied by Bill and Lynne Hybels
• Too Close Too Soon by Jim Talley, Bobbie Reed
• Finding Your Soulmate without Losing Your Head by Richard and Shirley Sexton
• I Kissed Dating Good-bye by Joshua Harris
• Boy Meets Girl: Say Hello to Courtship by Joshua Harris
• Should We Get Married by William P. Smith
• Who Should I Date by Jayne Clark, New Growth Press
• Watch and Pray: Red Flags in Christian Dating by Ernest Jefferson

Engagement
• IMarriage by Andy Stanley
• Sacred Marriage by Gary Thomas
• Real Marriage by Mark Driscoll
• Before You Get Engaged by David Gudgel and Brent Gudgel
• Before You Say "I Do": A Marriage Preparation Manual for Couples by Norman Wright, Wes Roberts
• 101 Questions to Ask before You Get Engaged by H. Norman Wright
• No Longer Two: A Christian Guide for Engagement and Marriage by Brian and Barbara Edwards
• The Marriage You've Always Dreamed Of... - The Marriage Preparation Manual for Young Christian Women by Mary Taylor Williamson

Divorce/Separation/Remarriage
Top 5 Books/Studies to read after you go through Divorce Recovery study
by Cloud and Townsend

1. How People Grow
2. Boundaries in general, dating, marriage again
3. Hiding From Love
4. Safe People
5. Changes that Heal
• Hope for New Relationships by Dr. Dennis Henderson
• Divorce and Remarriage by Dr. Tony Evans
• Daily Devotion for Single Mom's by Crosswalk.com. Subscribe today!
• When "I Do" Becomes "I Don't" by Laura Petherbridge
• Divorce Care: Hope, Help and Healing During and After Your Divorce by Kathy Leonard
• Before You Remarry by H. Norman Wright (workbook)
• Growing in Remarriage: Seven Keys to a Successful Second Marriage by Jim Smoke
• Hope for the Separated: Wounded Marriages Can Be Healed by Gary D. Chapman
• When the Vow Breaks: A Survival and Recovery Guide for Christians Facing Divorce by Joseph Warren Kniskern
• The Single Again Handbook: Finding Meaning and Fulfillment When You're Single Again by Thomas Jones
• Counseling and Divorce by Davd A. Thompson (resources for christian counseling)
• Counseling Families After Divorce by David R. Miller
• The Fresh Start Divorce Recovery Workbook:
  A Step-by-Step Program for Those Who Are Divorced Or Separated by Tom Whiteman, Bob Burns
• Beginning Again by Terry Hershey
• Growing Through Divorce by Jim Smoke
• Dare to Trust, Dare to Hope Again: Living With Losses of the Heart by Kari West
• Help for Parents of a Divorced Son or Daughter by Harold Ivan Smith

• Starting Over by Jayne Clark

Blended/Singles Parenting Families
• The Daddy Gap by Dawn Walker and Matt Haviland
• A Fathers Walk by Matt Haviland
• Single Parenting That Works: Six Keys to Raising Happy, Healthy Children in a Single-Parent Home by Kevin Leman
• Loving Your Step Family by Dr. Don Partridge
• Attract Families to Your Church and Keep Them Coming Back by Linda Jacobs
• The Single Mom and Her Roller Coaster Emotions by Pam Kanaly
• Any book by Kevin Leman
• Dating and the Single Parent by Ron Deal
• The Single Mom's Devotional: A Book of 52 Practical and Encouraging Devotions by Carol Finch
• Peace and the SIngle Mom by Jennifer Maggio (new)
• The Single Dad's Survival Guide: How to Succeed as a One-Man Parenting Team - eBook by Michael A. Klumpp
• The Smart Step Family by Ron Deal
• Financial Relief for Single Parents: A Proven Plan for Achieving the Seemingly Impossible by Brenda Armstrong
• Dating and the Single Parent by Ron Deal
• Co-Parenting Works! Working Together to Help Your Children Thrive by Tammy Daughtry
• Help, I am Raising My Kids Alone by T.D. Jakes
• New Start for Singles Mom's Starter Kit by Diane Strack
• Parenting On Your Own by Lynda Hunter
• Your Step-family Standing Strong (CD's) by Ron Deal and Dennis Rainey
• Life in a Blender: Booklet for Teens before and after their parents remarry by Ron Deal
• My Mommy is Getting Married by Pam Chambers

• When Your Parent Remarries Late in Life: Making Peace with Your Adult Stepfamily by Terri P. Smith
• Resolving Conflict in the Blended Family by Tom Frydenger, Adrienne Frydenger
• The Smart Step-Mom by Laura Petherbridge
• Singles Parents: The Hardest Job by Robert D. Jones
• From One Single Mother to Another: Heart-Lifting Encouragement and Practical Advice by Sandra P. Aldrich

Grief and Loss
• Caring for Widows: You and Your Church Can Make a Difference by Wesley M. Teterud
• Comforting the Bereaved: For Pastors and Others Who Minister by Warren W. Wiersbe, David W. Wiersbe
• Griefshare: Bible study by Church Initiative
• Grieving the Death of a Mother by Harold Ivan Smith (Harold has a several books dealing with grief.)
• Experiencing Grief by H. Norman Wright

Cohabitating
• Living Together: Myths, Risks & Answers by Mike McManus, Harriett McManus, Chuck Colson• The Ring Makes All the Difference: The Hidden Consequences of Cohabitation and the Strong Benefits of Marriage by Glenn T. Stanton

Counseling
• Help for the Post-Abortion Woman by Teri K Reisser, Paul Reisser
• The Emotionally Destructive Relationship by Leslie Vernick
• Boundaries by Henry Cloud
• Safe People by Cloud and Townsend
• Counseling Single Adults: A Handbook of Principles and Advice by Douglas L. Fagerstrom, Jim Smoke

- Counseling Before Marriage by Everett L. Worthington, Gary R. Collins
- Counseling and Homosexuality by Earl B. Wilson
- The Bondage Breaker by Neil Anderson
- Approval Addiction by Joyce Meyer
- Weight of Grace by Paula Neall Coleman (prefer small group study)
- Bod 4 God by Pastor Steve Reynolds (individual or small group)
- New Growth Press (several books/studies on counseling)
- A Woman Who Hurts; A God Who Heals by Elsa Kok

Sexuality
- Sex and The Single Christian by Barry Colman
- Let's Talk About Sex and Relationships by Tania Vaughn
- Singled Out by Christine Colon & Bonnie Field
- Surfing for God Audio Book by Michale John Cusick
- Love is an Orientation by Andrew Marin
- Sex and The Single Purpose by Bob DeMoss
- Your Single Treasure by Rick Stedman
- The War Within by Robert Daniels
- Every Single Mans Battle (workbook) Several Authors
- Every Woman's Battle by Several Authors
- Sex is Not the Problem, Lust Is by Joshua Harris
- No More Sheets: The Truth About Sex by Juanita Bynum
- Sex Before Marriage by Timothy Lane

Finance
- Dollars & Uncommon Sense: Basic Training for Your Money Paperback by Steve Repak
- Every Single Cent by Larry Burkett and Brenda Armstrong - Guide/Bible study to help singles with budgeting.
- Financial Relief for Singles Parents by Brenda Armstrong -

Guide to help single parents budget.
• The Everything Guide to Personal Finance for Single Mothers by Susan. Reynolds and Robert Bexton
• Crosswalk Online Magazine: Ton of great articles to help in this area of budgeting as a single.
• Anything by Dave Ramsey
• Money and Faith in Motion by ACCE - A great resource to manage, budget and use of your finances.

Single Life (Purpose, Contentment, Personal Walk)
• How to Develop a Powerful Prayer Life by Dr. Gregory Frizzel
• Living Whole Without a Better HalfBiblical Truth for the Single Life by Wendy Widder
• If Singleness Is a Gift, What's the Return Policy by Michelle McKinny Hammond, Holly VIrden
• Singled Out by Christine Colon & Bonnie Field
• Living Every Single Moment by Angela Payne
• Being Single and Satisfied by Tony Evans
• The 10 Best Decisions a Single Can Make by Bill Farrel
• Table for One by Camerin Courtney
• The Joy of Being Saved and Single by Lawrence Moore and Shelley Jones
• The Singles Christian Woman's Fight for Focus by Sherabim Allen
• Single Adults Want to Be the Church, Too by Britton Wood
• Common Mistakes Singles Make by Mary S. Whelchel
• For Single Men and Women by John Piper (online book)
• Redeeming Singleness by Barry Danylak
• The Single WomanLife, Love, and a Dash of Sassy by Mandy Hale
• God's Call to the Single Adult by Michael Cavanaugh
• Sassy, Single & Satisfied by Michelle McKinney Hammond
• Single and Loving It by Kate McVeigh

- Heloise Household Hints for Singles by Heloise
- Holy Me? The Single Adult's Guide to the Spiritual Journey by Harold Ivan Smith
- Living Whole With a Better Half by Wendy Widder
- Single but Not Alone by Jane Graver
- It's Not All about You: Young Adults Seeking Justice by Julie Richardson Brown and Courtney Richards
- Singled Out For Him by Nancy Leigh DeMoss
- Singles at the Crossroads by Albert Y. Hsu
- Being Single in the Church Today by Philip Wilson
- Who Has Your Heart by Emily E. Ryan
- Live Like You Mean It by Kathy Troccoli

NOTE: Use this space to list other resources as you discover them.

ENCLOSURE 1

MARITAL STATUS

2010 American Community Survey 1-Year Estimates

Although the American Community Survey (ACS) produces population, demographic and housing unit estimates, for 2010, the 2010 Census provides the official counts of the population and housing units for the nation, states, counties, cities and towns.

| | United States | | | | | | | | | | | |
| | Total | | Now married (except separated) | | Widowed | | Divorced | | Separated | | Never married | |
Subject	Estimate	Margin of Error	Estimate	Margin of Error	Estimate	Margin of Error	Estimate	Margin of Error	Estimate	Margin of Error	Estimate	Margin of Error
Population 15 years and over	248,055,946	+/- 35,568	48.8%	+/- 0.1	6.0%	+/- 0.1	10.9%	+/- 0.1	2.2%	+/- 0.1	32.1%	+/- 0.1
AGE AND SEX												
Males 15 years and over	120,742,609	+/- 25,786	50.5%	+/- 0.1	2.5%	+/- 0.1	9.6%	+/- 0.1	1.9%	+/- 0.1	35.4%	+/- 0.1
15 to 19 years	11,352,610	+/- 24,833	0.7%	+/- 0.1	0.0%	+/- 0.1	0.0%	+/- 0.1	0.1%	+/- 0.1	99.2%	+/- 0.1
20 to 34 years	31,638,358	+/- 31,251	29.4%	+/- 0.2	0.1%	+/- 0.1	3.5%	+/- 0.1	1.4%	+/- 0.1	65.6%	+/- 0.2
35 to 44 years	20,494,598	+/- 23,430	61.7%	+/- 0.2	0.4%	+/- 0.1	11.7%	+/- 0.1	2.9%	+/- 0.1	23.3%	+/- 0.2
45 to 54 years	22,100,095	+/- 21,716	64.4%	+/- 0.2	1.0%	+/- 0.1	16.0%	+/- 0.1	2.8%	+/- 0.1	15.8%	+/- 0.1
55 to 64 years	17,723,303	+/- 12,075	70.0%	+/- 0.1	2.5%	+/- 0.1	16.2%	+/- 0.1	2.2%	+/- 0.1	9.2%	+/- 0.1
65 years and over	17,433,645	+/- 10,862	70.9%	+/- 0.2	13.1%	+/- 0.1	9.9%	+/- 0.1	1.3%	+/- 0.1	4.7%	+/- 0.1
Females 15 years and over	127,313,337	+/- 27,921	47.1%	+/- 0.1	9.3%	+/- 0.1	12.1%	+/- 0.1	2.5%	+/- 0.1	29.0%	+/- 0.1
15 to 19 years	10,751,573	+/- 28,890	1.5%	+/- 0.1	0.0%	+/- 0.1	0.1%	+/- 0.1	0.1%	+/- 0.1	98.3%	+/- 0.1
20 to 34 years	30,996,555	+/- 26,162	36.7%	+/- 0.2	0.2%	+/- 0.1	5.0%	+/- 0.1	2.5%	+/- 0.1	55.6%	+/- 0.2
35 to 44 years	20,697,730	+/- 17,567	62.5%	+/- 0.2	1.0%	+/- 0.1	14.2%	+/- 0.1	4.3%	+/- 0.1	18.0%	+/- 0.1
45 to 54 years	22,828,938	+/- 16,851	62.3%	+/- 0.2	3.1%	+/- 0.1	18.9%	+/- 0.2	3.7%	+/- 0.1	12.1%	+/- 0.1
55 to 64 years	19,038,661	+/- 13,080	61.2%	+/- 0.2	8.4%	+/- 0.1	19.8%	+/- 0.1	2.6%	+/- 0.1	8.0%	+/- 0.1
65 years and over	22,999,880	+/- 13,663	41.6%	+/- 0.2	40.4%	+/- 0.1	12.3%	+/- 0.1	1.0%	+/- 0.1	4.7%	+/- 0.1
Population 15 years and over	248,055,946	+/- 35,568	48.8%	+/- 0.1	6.0%	+/- 0.1	10.9%	+/- 0.1	2.2%	+/- 0.1	32.1%	+/- 0.1
RACE AND HISPANIC OR LATINO ORIGIN												
One race	243,087,762	+/- 47,953	49.0%	+/- 0.1	6.1%	+/- 0.1	10.9%	+/- 0.1	2.2%	+/- 0.1	31.8%	+/- 0.1
White	187,768,002	+/- 94,414	52.1%	+/- 0.1	6.4%	+/- 0.1	11.3%	+/- 0.1	1.8%	+/- 0.1	28.4%	+/- 0.1
Black or African American	30,106,985	+/- 32,637	29.3%	+/- 0.2	5.9%	+/- 0.1	12.1%	+/- 0.1	4.4%	+/- 0.1	48.3%	+/- 0.2
American Indian and Alaska Native	1,944,873	+/- 22,901	36.8%	+/- 0.7	4.7%	+/- 0.2	13.2%	+/- 0.4	3.0%	+/- 0.2	42.3%	+/- 0.7

Subject	Total Estimate	Margin of Error	Now married (except separated) Estimate	Margin of Error	Widowed Estimate	Margin of Error	Divorced Estimate	Margin of Error	Separated Estimate	Margin of Error	Never married Estimate	Margin of Error
Asian	12,018,513	+/- 22,984	57.9%	+/- 0.3	4.4%	+/- 0.1	5.1%	+/- 0.1	1.3%	+/- 0.1	31.3%	+/- 0.2
Native Hawaiian and Other Pacific Islander	384,493	+/-7,713	46.1%	+/- 1.2	3.8%	+/- 0.4	8.0%	+/- 0.8	2.4%	+/- 0.5	39.7%	+/- 1.3
Some other race	10,864,896	+/- 82,178	43.0%	+/- 0.3	2.5%	+/- 0.1	7.3%	+/- 0.2	3.6%	+/- 0.1	43.6%	+/- 0.3
Two or more races	4,968,184	+/- 54,785	35.5%	+/- 0.4	3.4%	+/- 0.1	10.5%	+/- 0.2	2.8%	+/- 0.1	47.9%	+/- 0.4
Hispanic or Latino origin (of any race)	36,230,874	+/- 15,689	44.2%	+/- 0.2	3.2%	+/- 0.1	8.2%	+/- 0.1	3.5%	+/- 0.1	40.9%	+/- 0.2
White alone, not Hispanic or Latino	164,472,657	+/- 16,187	53.0%	+/- 0.1	6.8%	+/- 0.1	11.7%	+/- 0.1	1.6%	+/- 0.1	26.9%	+/- 0.1
NATIVITY												
Native	210,073,883	+/- 126,243	47.0%	+/- 0.1	6.2%	+/- 0.1	11.5%	+/- 0.1	2.1%	+/- 0.1	33.2%	+/- 0.1
Foreign born	37,982,063	+/- 105,748	58.5%	+/- 0.2	5.1%	+/- 0.1	7.5%	+/- 0.1	3.1%	+/- 0.1	25.8%	+/- 0.2
LABOR FORCE PARTICIPATION												
Males 16 years and over	118,561,135	+/- 31,795	51.5%	+/- 0.1	2.6%	+/- 0.1	9.8%	+/- 0.1	1.9%	+/- 0.1	34.2%	+/- 0.1
In labor force	82,736,110	+/- 79,299	55.2%	+/- 0.1	0.9%	+/- 0.1	9.5%	+/- 0.1	2.0%	+/- 0.1	32.4%	+/- 0.1
Females 16 years and over	125,271,788	+/- 35,525	47.8%	+/- 0.1	9.5%	+/- 0.1	12.3%	+/- 0.1	2.6%	+/- 0.1	27.8%	+/- 0.1
In labor force	74,230,659	+/- 86,750	49.3%	+/- 0.1	3.0%	+/- 0.1	14.1%	+/- 0.1	3.0%	+/- 0.1	30.7%	+/- 0.1
PERCENT IMPUTED												
Marital status	3.0%	(X)	(X)	(X)	(X)	(X)	(X)	(X)	(X)	(X)	(X)	(X)

Source: U.S. Census Bureau, 2010 American Community Survey

Explanation of Symbols:

1. An '**' entry in the margin of error column indicates that either no sample observations or too few sample

observations were available to compute a standard error and thus the margin of error. A statistical test is not appropriate.

2.   An '-' entry in the estimate column indicates that either no sample observations or too few sample observations were available to compute an estimate, or a ratio of medians cannot be calculated because one or both of the median estimates falls in the lowest interval or upper interval of an open-ended distribution.

3.   An '-' following a median estimate means the median falls in the lowest interval of an open-ended distribution.

4.   An '+' following a median estimate means the median falls in the upper interval of an open-ended distribution.

5.   An '***' entry in the margin of error column indicates that the median falls in the lowest interval or upper interval of an open-ended distribution. A statistical test is not appropriate.

6.   An '*****' entry in the margin of error column indicates that the estimate is controlled. A statistical test for sampling variability is not appropriate.

7.   An 'N' entry in the estimate and margin of error columns indicates that data for this geographic area cannot be displayed because the number of sample cases is too small.

8.   An '(X)' means that the estimate is not applicable or not available.

NOTES:

HOLT & STEPHENS

ENCLOSURE 2

Table 4.
Households and Families for the United States, Regions, States, and for Puerto Rico: 2000 and 2010
(For information on confidentiality protection, nonsampling errors, and definitions, see www.census.gov/prod/cen2010/doc/sf1.pdf)

Area	All households		Family households						Nonfamily households			Average number of people in 2010	
			Husband-wife households		Female family households¹		Male family households¹		One person				
	April 1, 2000	April 1, 2010	Total	With own children under 18 years	Total	With own children under 18 years	Total	With own children under 18 years	Total	With householder 65 years and over	Two or more people	Per household	Per family
United States ...	105,480,101	116,716,292	48.4	20.2	13.1	7.2	5.0	2.4	26.7	9.4	6.8	2.58	3.14
REGION													
Northeast..........	20,285,622	21,215,415	46.9	19.5	13.3	6.9	4.7	2.1	28.1	10.7	7.0	2.53	3.12
Midwest..........	24,734,532	26,215,951	48.8	19.7	11.9	6.9	4.6	2.4	28.1	10.1	6.5	2.49	3.06
South..............	38,015,214	43,609,929	48.3	19.7	14.2	7.8	4.9	2.3	26.4	9.0	6.3	2.56	3.10
West	22,444,733	25,674,997	49.5	22.1	12.2	6.6	5.6	2.8	24.8	8.4	8.0	2.74	3.30
STATE													
Alabama	1,737,080	1,883,791	47.9	18.5	15.3	8.1	4.6	2.0	27.4	9.8	4.8	2.48	3.02
Alaska	221,600	258,058	49.4	22.7	10.7	6.8	6.0	3.5	25.6	5.4	8.2	2.65	3.21
Arizona	1,901,327	2,380,990	48.1	19.5	12.4	7.1	5.6	3.0	26.1	9.1	7.7	2.63	3.19
Arkansas	1,042,696	1,147,084	49.5	18.9	13.4	7.7	4.7	2.4	27.1	10.1	5.3	2.47	3.00
California	11,502,870	12,577,498	49.4	23.4	13.3	6.8	6.0	2.8	23.3	8.1	8.0	2.90	3.45
Colorado	1,658,238	1,972,868	49.2	21.4	10.1	6.0	4.6	2.5	27.9	7.8	8.1	2.49	3.08
Connecticut	1,301,670	1,371,087	49.0	20.9	12.9	7.1	4.4	1.9	27.3	10.6	6.5	2.52	3.08
Delaware	298,736	342,297	48.3	18.3	14.2	7.6	5.0	2.4	25.6	9.7	7.0	2.55	3.06
District of Columbia ...	248,338	266,707	22.0	7.9	16.4	7.9	3.9	1.3	44.0	9.7	13.7	2.11	3.01
Florida	6,337,929	7,420,802	46.6	16.6	13.5	7.1	5.0	2.3	27.2	11.1	7.6	2.48	3.01
Georgia	3,006,369	3,585,584	47.8	21.1	15.8	8.9	4.9	2.2	25.4	7.5	6.1	2.63	3.17
Hawaii	403,240	455,338	50.5	20.1	12.6	5.2	5.8	2.4	23.3	8.1	7.7	2.89	3.42
Idaho	469,645	579,408	55.3	24.0	9.6	5.9	4.7	2.8	23.8	8.8	6.6	2.66	3.16
Illinois.............	4,591,779	4,836,972	48.2	21.0	12.9	6.9	4.7	2.2	27.8	9.7	6.4	2.59	3.20
Indiana............	2,336,306	2,502,154	49.6	19.9	12.4	7.3	4.9	2.6	26.9	9.5	6.2	2.52	3.05
Iowa..............	1,149,276	1,221,576	51.2	20.0	9.3	5.9	4.2	2.5	28.4	11.1	6.9	2.41	2.97
Kansas............	1,037,891	1,112,096	51.1	21.3	10.4	6.5	4.5	2.6	27.8	9.9	6.2	2.49	3.06
Kentucky	1,590,647	1,719,965	49.3	19.1	12.7	7.1	4.8	2.4	27.5	9.8	5.6	2.45	2.98
Louisiana	1,656,053	1,728,360	44.4	17.6	17.2	9.3	5.5	2.6	26.9	8.9	6.0	2.55	3.10
Maine..............	518,200	557,219	48.5	16.7	10.0	6.0	4.5	2.7	28.6	11.3	8.4	2.32	2.83
Maryland	1,980,859	2,156,411	47.6	20.4	14.6	7.6	4.8	2.2	26.1	8.7	6.8	2.61	3.15
Massachusetts......	2,443,580	2,547,075	46.3	19.7	12.5	6.8	4.2	1.8	28.7	10.6	8.3	2.48	3.08
Michigan	3,785,661	3,872,508	48.0	18.9	13.2	7.3	4.8	2.4	27.9	10.2	6.2	2.49	3.05
Minnesota	1,895,127	2,087,227	50.8	21.2	9.5	5.9	4.3	2.3	28.0	9.7	7.4	2.48	3.05
Mississippi..........	1,046,434	1,115,768	45.4	17.8	18.5	10.0	5.2	2.4	26.3	9.5	4.6	2.58	3.11
Missouri	2,194,594	2,375,611	48.4	18.9	12.3	7.1	4.6	2.5	28.3	10.1	6.4	2.45	3.00
Montana............	358,667	409,607	49.2	17.8	9.0	5.4	4.5	2.6	29.7	10.7	7.5	2.35	2.91
Nebraska..........	666,184	721,130	50.8	21.2	9.8	6.2	4.2	2.3	28.7	10.4	6.5	2.46	3.04
Nevada	751,165	1,006,250	46.0	19.6	12.7	7.0	6.6	3.3	25.7	7.9	9.1	2.65	3.20
New Hampshire......	474,606	518,973	52.1	20.4	9.7	5.7	4.5	2.5	25.6	9.2	8.0	2.46	2.96
New Jersey	3,064,645	3,214,360	51.1	23.3	13.3	6.6	4.8	2.0	25.2	10.1	5.5	2.68	3.22
New Mexico	677,971	791,395	45.3	17.9	14.0	7.8	6.2	3.4	28.0	9.3	6.5	2.55	3.13
New York	7,056,860	7,317,755	43.6	18.7	14.9	7.5	5.0	2.1	29.1	10.5	7.3	2.57	3.20
North Carolina......	3,132,013	3,745,155	48.4	19.6	13.7	7.8	4.6	2.3	27.0	9.1	6.3	2.48	3.01
North Dakota........	257,152	281,192	48.6	18.6	8.2	5.2	4.1	2.2	31.5	11.0	7.7	2.30	2.91
Ohio..............	4,445,773	4,603,435	47.2	18.2	13.1	7.5	4.7	2.4	28.9	10.4	6.2	2.44	3.01
Oklahoma	1,342,293	1,460,450	49.5	19.7	12.3	7.0	5.0	2.7	27.5	9.9	5.8	2.49	3.04
Oregon............	1,333,723	1,518,938	48.3	18.7	10.5	6.1	4.7	2.5	27.4	9.7	9.1	2.47	3.00
Pennsylvania	4,777,003	5,018,904	48.2	18.3	12.2	6.5	4.6	2.2	28.6	11.4	6.5	2.45	3.02
Rhode Island........	408,424	413,600	44.5	17.6	13.5	7.7	4.8	2.2	29.5	11.3	7.6	2.44	3.04
South Carolina......	1,533,854	1,801,181	47.2	17.7	15.6	8.4	4.7	2.2	26.5	9.2	5.9	2.49	3.01
South Dakota........	290,245	322,282	50.1	19.7	9.7	6.2	4.4	2.6	29.4	10.9	6.4	2.42	3.00
Tennessee..........	2,232,905	2,493,552	48.7	18.7	13.9	7.5	4.8	2.3	26.9	9.4	5.7	2.48	3.01
Texas..............	7,393,354	8,922,933	50.6	23.7	14.1	8.0	5.2	2.5	24.2	7.2	5.9	2.75	3.31
Utah..............	701,281	877,692	61.0	31.7	9.7	5.5	4.4	2.2	18.7	6.4	6.1	3.10	3.56
Vermont............	240,634	256,442	48.5	17.6	9.6	6.0	4.4	2.6	28.2	10.3	9.3	2.34	2.85
Virginia..........	2,699,173	3,056,058	50.2	21.1	12.4	6.7	4.4	2.0	26.0	8.5	7.0	2.54	3.06
Washington	2,271,398	2,620,076	49.2	20.4	10.5	6.2	4.7	2.5	27.2	8.7	8.4	2.51	3.06
West Virginia........	736,481	763,831	49.8	17.0	11.2	5.7	4.8	2.3	28.4	11.6	5.8	2.36	2.88
Wisconsin..........	2,084,544	2,279,768	49.6	19.4	10.3	6.4	4.5	2.5	28.2	10.2	7.4	2.43	2.99
Wyoming	193,608	226,879	50.9	19.6	8.9	5.6	4.8	2.8	28.0	8.8	7.4	2.42	2.96
Puerto Rico	1,261,325	1,376,531	45.0	18.2	22.6	10.9	5.5	2.2	23.8	9.5	3.1	2.68	3.17

¹ No spouse present in household.
Sources: U.S. Census Bureau, Census 2000 Summary File 1 and 2010 Census Summary File 1.

U.S. Census Bureau

Table 5.

Top Ten Places of 100,000 or More Population With the Highest Percentage of One-Person Households: 2010

(For information on confidentiality protection, nonsampling errors, and definitions, see *www.census.gov/prod/cen2010/doc/sf1.pdf*)

Place[1]	Total households	One-person households		With householder 65 years and over	
		Number	Percent of total	Number	Percent of one-person households
Atlanta city, Georgia................	185,142	81,555	44.0	15,832	19.4
Washington city, District of Columbia	266,707	117,431	44.0	25,913	22.1
Cincinnati city, Ohio................	133,420	57,941	43.4	13,230	22.8
Alexandria city, Virginia	68,082	29,564	43.4	4,882	16.5
St. Louis city, Missouri................	142,057	60,468	42.6	14,424	23.9
Pittsburgh city, Pennsylvania...........	136,217	56,823	41.7	16,469	29.0
Arlington CDP, Virginia...............	98,050	40,516	41.3	6,523	16.1
Seattle city, Washington...............	283,510	117,054	41.3	24,611	21.0
Cambridge city, Massachusetts.........	44,032	17,933	40.7	4,242	23.7
Denver city, Colorado................	263,107	106,828	40.6	23,686	22.2

[1] The 2010 Census showed 282 places in the United States with 100,000 or more population. They included 273 incorporated places (including 5 city-county consolidations) and 9 census designated places (CDPs) that were not legally incorporated.

Source: U.S. Census Bureau, *2010 Census Summary File 1.*

maintained only 22 percent of households in the District of Columbia. Regional patterns in the proportion of husband-wife households show that the highest percentage was in the West (50 percent) while the lowest percentage was in the Northeast (47 percent).

Over a quarter of households were one-person households.

In 2010, 31.2 million households consisted of one person living alone.[12] This represents a 4.0 million increase in one-person households since 2000. Although this increase from 2000 to 2010 was smaller than the growth experienced between 1990 and 2000 (4.6 million), the proportion of one-person households grew slightly from 26 percent in 2000 to 27 percent in 2010. About one-third of

all one-person households in 2010 had householders who were 65 years and over, compared with 22 percent of all householders (Table 1).

Table 5 shows the top ten places with the highest proportion of one-person households and the percentage of these households maintained by a person 65 and older. In 2010, one-person households were the most common form of household type in Atlanta, Georgia, and Washington, DC (both 44 percent), followed by St. Louis, Missouri; Cincinnati, Ohio; and Alexandria, Virginia, with 43 percent. People over the age of 65 occupied less than 20 percent of one-person households in Atlanta; Arlington, Virginia; and Alexandria. These areas may represent cities inhabited by younger adults who may move in search of job opportunities.

Figures 3a, 3b, and 3c are maps showing the percentage of one-person households and their geographical concentration at the county level.[13] Figure 3a shows a high percentage of one-person households concentrated along the upper and central Midwest extending down into northeastern New Mexico. Figure 3b shows a much smaller proportion of Midwestern counties with high concentrations of persons living alone for those aged 15 to 64 years. Figure 3c specifically examines one-person households composed of individuals 65 years and older. It shows that the high percentages noted in Figure 3a in the Midwest are the result of the elderly living alone, perhaps staying in or not moving far from homes or towns where

[12] One-person households are a subset of nonfamily households. In one-person households the householder lives alone.

[13] A reference to state includes states and their statistically equivalent entities. A reference to county includes counties and their statistically equivalent entities.

ENCLOSURE 3

Hilldale Baptist Church
S.P.L.A.S.H. Leadership Team Covenant

S.P.L.A.S.H. (Single People Loving And Serving Him)
 Purpose: **To reach and teach *Single People* about Jesus, leading them to accept a *Loving* relationship in Christ *And* equipping them to *Serve Him*. To help single people discover God's Calling in their lives and encourage them to pursue it.**

Having received Christ as my Savior and Lord and having been scripturally baptized I now desire to become a part of the S.P.L.A.S.H. Leadership Team. In doing so I commit myself to God and to others to support the S.P.L.A.S.H. Purpose by doing the following:

1. I WILL PROTECT THE UNITY OF S.P.L.A.S.H. & THE CHURCH...
> ...By acting in love toward others in S.P.L.A.S.H. and the church.
> ...By refusing to gossip and discouraging from doing so.
> ...By following the spiritual leadership of others.

2. I WILL SHARE IN THE RESPONSIBILITY FOR S.P.L.A.S.H....
> ...By praying for its growth.
> ...By inviting other single people to attend, especially the un-churched.
> ...By warmly welcoming our guests.

3. I WILL SERVE THE SINGLE ADULT MINISTRY...
> ...By discovering my gifts and talents and seeking to use them.
> ...By allowing other S.P.L.A.S.H. leaders to equip me to serve in ministry.
> ...By seeking to develop a servant's heart.

4. I WILL GUARD THE TESTIMONY OF S.P.L.A.S.H., THE CHURCH & MYSELF...
> ...By faithfully attending Sunday School and Worship, and other activities
> > as time allows.

...By living a consecrated Godly life, including sexual purity in my
   relationships and refusing to use substances, such as alcohol, or
go
   places which call into question my testimony as a Christian.
...By Biblical financial support of the church.

**5. I WILL ATTEND EVERY LEADERSHIP TRAINING SESSION
   UNLESS UNAVOIDABLY HINDERED AND DO THE WORK
   ASSIGNED IN ORDER TO GROW AS A LEADER..**

Signature_____

Date_____

ENCLOSURE 4

SINGLE ADULT SURVEY

Today's Date...

Thanks for taking a few moments to complete this survey.
Your answers will help our ministry to better meet your needs.

(Circle One)   Male   Female
If you want your name & telephone in the Singles Phone
Directory please complete the name & address section below.
NAME...
ADDRESS...
TELEPHONE (HOME)...
(WORK)..
E-MAIL...
(FAX)...

1. Describe Your Occupation:
....

Military Status - Active Duty?..........
If so, what Unit?....................................
    Retired?...................

2. Current Status:
 ..... Never Been Married
 ..... Single Parent/Custodial
 ..... Single Parent/NonCustodial
 ..... Widow/Widower
 ..... Separated
 ..... Divorced

3. Check as many as apply:
.....I live with my child/children who are ages...............
.....I live with my parent(s).
.....I live with friend(s).
.....I live alone.
Special Needs?
(Disabilities)...

4. Age Category .....Under 20 .....20s .....30s 40s
.....50s   .....60s+

5. Church Participation:
.....I am a member of a Sunday School class here but NOT a
church member.
.....I have officially joined Hilldale Baptist Church.
.....I do not attend church
.....I regularly attend this church but have not joined.
.....I am a member or attend a Single Adult Class/Group at
another church.
          (Name of church)...
.....Describe any other outside Bible Studies you
attend.............................
..... Check here if you more information about your church and
the Single Adult Ministry.
          (List name/address at top of survey)
.....Please add me to your mailing list. (List name/address at
top of survey)
.....I am interested in being more involved: Please contact me.
(List name/address above)

6. If you have attended one of our Single adult groups, classes
or functions, what have you enjoyed MOST or LEAST about
them?

7. If you are considering NOT returning to our Single Adult Ministry, what would it take to change your mind?

8. Please check the needs and interests, you would most like to see within the Single Adult Ministry.   Add any of interest that we didn't include.
....Marriage Preperation
....Remarriage
....Spiritual Growth
....Goal Setting/Life Planning
....Personal Financial Planning
....Legal Issues
....Leadership Training
....Other (Specify) ....
....Sexuality/Intimacy
....Relationship Issues
....Health/Dieting
....Divorce Recovery
....Single Parenting
....Job/Career Change
....Success
....Time Management
....Blending Families
....Grief Recovery
....Stress Management
....Ministry Teams (list ministry)................
....Mission Trip/Work Group
Comments:

9. What do you think the PURPOSE of a Single Adult group should be?

11. How could our ministry best meet your needs?

12. The Bible says that we have all "sinned and fallen short of God's plan," (Romans 3:23), that God loved us enough that "while we were sinners, Christ died for us," (Romans 5:8) and that if you "confess with your mouth that Jesus is Lord and believe in your heart that God raised Him from the dead, you will be saved." (Romans 10:9) It is through acknowledging our sin, confessing it to God and asking Jesus to save us that we become Christians. Have you ever done that? .... Would you like for someone to explain it in more detail? ......

13. With your needs in mind, are there any other comments or insights we could benefit from as we develop this Single Adult Ministry?

14. Identify the top 5 issues Single Adults face today.

ENCLOSURE 5

Single Adult Ministry Report

_____ Church

To: Pastor, Finance Committee, Personnel Committee, Chairman of Deacons

<u>Year in Review</u> (Modify this format to fit your ministry or situation)

The (2001) year was an exciting one for our Single Adult Ministry. The statistics below provide details about our ministry for the year and compile them with previous years. Single adults continue to be vital to the ministry of our church just as we provide vital community to them. The divorce rate (12.5%) of those married here is still too high for me but it continues to remain well below the rate for our area (52%). The divorce rate for those who went through our pre-marriage counseling is currently 2.1%! Relationship training and marriage preparation will continue to be a high priority for our ministry.

* ___ saved/baptized into church membership (___ total including previous years)

* ___ joined by letter (___ total including previous years)

* ___ married (____ total including previous years)

* ___ transferred into Married Division (___ total including previous years)

* ___ trained and moved into Sunday morning leadership (___ total serving now)

* ___ teaching/leading in other ministries (___ total including previous years)

* ___ in Success/Relationship seminars this last year (___ total including previous years)

* ___ involved in Divorce and Relationship Recovery and in Single Parent Seminars (___ total including previous years)

* ___ in the choir and orchestra weekly

* ___ graduated from the personal empowerment training.

* ___ total current ministry teams ___ total active on those teams

* ___ new SS classes started (or ministries started) (___ started since I got here)

* ___ average Sunday School attendance. (____ average when I started)

* ___ average attendance for all weekly Bible Studies, including Sunday School

Dreams and Goals (be creative, set realistic goals that impact lives)

1. Now that Self-Directed Ministry Teams have been established and are being used by single adults to minister to each other, I am praying that the changes I see in them will translate into deeper spiritual growth individually and collectively. I dream of training __ additional single adults next year and see the formation of additional ministry teams as needs arise inside and outside the church.

2. An expanded Military Ministry which reaches more single soldiers; a possible partnership with the new Soldier Support Center.

3. A weekly television show targeted to reach young adults.

4. ___ new Sunday School classes to facilitate growth.

5. A ministry with Single Parents that reaches those in the community.

6. ____ Single Adults in regular Sunday School attendance.

7. A week night Bible Study in at least ___ apartment facilities.

8. Train 10% of Sunday School attendees to leave their class and provide Sunday morning leadership in other areas of the church.

Summary

God has richly blessed our Single Adult Ministry. I have committed myself to deeper spiritual growth and to grow in my leadership and management skills. I and our leaders want to keep before us and our members the vision of approximately _____ single adults in our area who are either unsaved or un-churched. I still use as my key ministry verse Joshua 3:5; "Sanctify yourselves: for tomorrow the Lord will do wonders among you."

Partners with you in Christ,

_____

Single Adult Leader

HOLT & STEPHENS

Enclosure 6: <u>Consolidated Contact Person List</u> – Reproduce this for your leaders

Association Phone _____
Contact Person _____

State Office phone _____
Contact Person _____

Prayer Team:
Name: _____
 Phone _____

Email _____

Name: _____
Phone _____

Email _____

Name: _____
Phone _____

Email _____

Name: _____
Phone _____

Email _____

Single Adults in your Church:

Name: _____
Phone _____

Email _____

Name: _____
Phone _____

Email _____

Name: _____
Phone _____

Email _____

Name: _____
Phone _____

Email _____

Church Leadership:

Pastor _____
Phone _____

Email _____

Other Staff _____

Phone _____

Email _____

Chairman of Deacons _____
Phone _____

Email_____

Finance Committee _____
Phone _____

Email_____

SAM Volunteers:

Name: _____
Phone _____

Email _____

Name: _____
Phone _____

Email _____

Name: _____
Phone _____

Email _____

Name: _____

HOLT & STEPHENS

Phone _____

Email _____

Local Counselors:

Name _____
Title _____

    Phone _____ **Accept Insurance?** _____
    Hourly Rate $ _____

    Name _____ **Title** _____

    Phone _____ **Accept Insurance?** _____

    Hourly Rate $ _____

Media List:

Media _____
Phone_____

Email_____

News Director _____
FAX No. _____

Call Letters (if applicable) _____
Radio frequency _____

Media _____

Phone_____

Email_____

News Director _____

FAX No. _____

Call Letters (if applicable) _____

Radio frequency _____

Media _____

Phone_____

Email_____

News Director _____

FAX No. _____

Call Letters (if applicable) _____

frequency _____

Media _____

Phone_____

Email_____

News Director _____

FAX No. _____

Call Letters (if applicable) _____

Radio frequency _____

Media _____

Phone_____

Email_____

News Director _____

FAX No. _____

Call Letters (if applicable) _____

Radio frequency _____

Media _____

Phone_____

Email_____

News Director _____

No. _____

Call Letters (if applicable) _____

Radio frequency _____

Start Day Area Leaders:

Teacher/Leader _____

Phone _____

Email _____

Setup _____

Phone _____

Email_____

Snacks/Food _____

Phone _____

Email_____

Greeters _____

Phone _____

Email _____

Follow up _____

Phone _____ _

Email _____

HOLT & STEPHENS

ENCLOSURE 7

Potential Leadership Team Member Assessment Profile
(Don't use this original...just make copies as needed.)

Name of potential Leader being evaluated:
_____

Name of Leader who is making this assessment:
_____

(Score the potential leader based on *YOUR* assessment of their strength in each of the areas below.)

Character-istic	Evaluation	Strongly Agree				Strongly Disagree
Spiritual	Demonstrates an interest in knowing God and His will for life	1	2	3	4	5
Creative	Shows the ability to be creative in performing ministry tasks	1	2	3	4	5
Team Player	Is dedicated to achieving the ministry team's goals	1	2	3	4	5
Humor	Maintains a sense of humor in times of pressure and difficulty	1	2	3	4	5
Responsible	Accepts responsibility for assigned ministry tasks and follows through until a project is completed	1	2	3	4	5
Respect	Receives support and respect from peers and coworkers	1	2	3	4	5
Skills	Expresses a desire to learn and develop new skills to complete the ministry task ahead	1	2	3	4	5
Cooperative	Demonstrates a cooperative spirit in working with others	1	2	3	4	5
Faithful	Is dedicated to the church's mission and is faithful to Jesus Christ	1	2	3	4	5
Decision making	Demonstrates sound judgment when facing decisions	1	2	3	4	5
Group participation	Expresses a desire to participate in special ministry projects, events, and retreats	1	2	3	4	5
Compassion	Cares about others and is sensitive to their needs	1	2	3	4	5
Risk taker	Demonstrates the courage to try something new by moving out of his or her comfort zone	1	2	3	4	5

We feel and recommend that potential leaders who *DO NOT* receive at least a '2' or a '1' in the areas of SPIRITUAL, RESPONSIBLE and FAITHFUL...***not*** be placed in leadership right away. They should be active in ongoing Leadership Training and be reassessed at a future date. If you place someone in a leadership position who *isn't* interested in knowing God or isn't responsible to follow through on SAM responsibilities or who isn't faithful to Jesus.....that area of your SAM is sure to fail. In all other areas the potential leader should receive a '3' or better before being given leadership responsibilities.

NEVER place someone in a leadership position simply because they are popular with singles in the group.

NOTES:

ABOUT THE AUTHORS

Max Holt

Max Holt was the Minister with Single Adults at Hilldale Baptist Church, Clarksville, Tennessee for 15 years, impacting the lives of thousands of single people in all life situations. He is currently a Single Adult Ministry Consultant for the Tennessee Baptist Convention in the areas of SAM Leadership and Empowerment issues. He is also the author of **Every Single Devotional,** a devotional book for single adults.

Max's Publishing Firm, MAX HOLT MEDIA, has a focus on publications that support the ministry to Christian Single Adults. The firm also publishes Christian-Friendly fiction for adults, down through young teens, mostly in the Science Fiction genre.

EVERY SINGLE MINISTRY, Leader Edition, was the first in his **EVERY SINGLE…. Series.** Books are planned addressing: Divorce, Finances, Single Parenting, Blended Families, Marriage Preparation, Cooking For One, Retirement, Single Women, Single Men, Relationships, and other subjects under development. The unique aspect of the EVERY SINGLE…Series is that every book will contain advice about the subject from other single people who have experienced the challenges in that area of life.

Prior to his ministry experience Max retired from a 22-year career in the U.S. Army. He may be contacted at max@maxholtmedia.com or via mobile at 731-819-4241.

HOLT & STEPHENS

Doug Stephens

Doug Stephens is a L.I.F.E. Group Leader for S.A.M. at Hilldale Baptist Church in Clarksville, Tennessee. He has over 30 years of experience at all levels of ministry leadership and partnered with Max Holt in SAM Leadership for 15 years at Hilldale Baptist. Doug has previous experience as a Seminar Leader and Empowerment Trainer for Lifeway Christian Resources at both the national and state levels. He and his wife Sara lead the DivorceCare Ministry at HBC.

Prior to his ministry experience Doug retired after a 20-year career in the U.S. Army. He may be contacted at sara.stephens@cdelightband.net. Or at
931-358-9601.

www.ingramcontent.com/pod-product-compliance
Lightning Source LLC
Chambersburg PA
CBHW080935040426
42443CB00015B/3425